FamilyFun
COOKING *with* KIDS

PAGE 205

FamilyFun
COOKING *with* KIDS

from the experts at FamilyFun Magazine

NEW YORK

FAMILYFUN

EDITORS
Deanna F. Cook
Grace Ganssle

COPY EDITOR
Eddy Goldberg

RESEARCH EDITOR
Kelly Coffey

EDITORIAL ASSISTANT
Miranda Becker

EDITORIAL INTERNS
Sarah Perkins
Annie Yoon

CONTRIBUTING
EDITORS
Dawn Chipman
Ann Hallock
Alexandra Kennedy
Gregory Lauzon
Cindy A. Littlefield

CONTRIBUTING
WRITER
Charlotte Meryman

TEST KITCHEN
Megan Hession
Alcestis Llobrera

PRODUCTION
Lauren Armstrong
Jennifer Mayer
Dana Stiepock

TECHNOLOGY
COORDINATOR
Thomas Lepper

IMPRESS, INC.

DESIGN
Pam Glaven
Hans Teensma, *Director*

This book is dedicated to the readers of *FamilyFun* magazine.

All of the ideas in this book first appeared in *FamilyFun* magazine. *FamilyFun* is a division of the Walt Disney Publishing Group. To order a subscription, call 800-289-4849.

The staffs of *FamilyFun* and Impress, Inc., conceived and produced *FamilyFun Cooking with Kids* at 47 Pleasant Street, Northampton, Massachusetts 01060, in collaboration with Disney Editions, 114 Fifth Avenue, New York, New York 10011-5690.

ABOUT THE EDITORS

DEANNA F. COOK, Creative Development Director of *FamilyFun* magazine, is the editor of the *FamilyFun* book series from Disney Editions, as well as the author of *The Kids' Multicultural Cookbook* from Williamson. She cooks in her Florence, Massachusetts, home with her husband, Doug, and their girls, Ella and Maisie.

GRACE GANSSLE, Associate Editor in the Creative Development group of *FamilyFun* magazine, is the former food and entertainment editor at *Disney Magazine*. She has cooked many of the meals in this book with her two sons, Paul and Andrew, in their Florence, Massachusetts, home.

KEN HAEDRICH, Contributing Editor for *FamilyFun* magazine, has developed many of the recipes in this book. He is a Julia Child Cookbook Award winner and the author of dozens of cookbooks. His titles include *Pie* and *Soup Makes the Meal* (both from Harvard Common Press).

ISBN 0-4231-0086-7

First Edition
10 9 8 7 6 5 4 3 2 1

Library of Congress Cataloging-in-Publication Data on file.
Printed in Malaysia

Acknowledgments

SPECIAL THANKS to the following *FamilyFun* magazine writers for their contributions: Vickie Lynn Agee, Barbara Albright, Barbara Beery, Lynne Bertrand, Anthony Dias Blue, Rebecca Boucher, Roberta Des Bouillons, Cynthia Caldwell, Marie Cecchini, Sharon Miller Cindrich, Joan Cirillo, Tobye Cook, Amy Cotler, Ellen Haas, Linda Gucia, Amy Hamel, Anne Hodgman, Linda Hopkins, Mollie Katzen, Joanne Kicza, Mary King, Kathy Farrell-Kingsley, Jeanne Lemlin, Frederick G. Levine, Julia Lynch, Shoshana Marchand, Elaine Magee, Colin McEnroe, Catherine Newman, Leslie Garisto Pfaff, Jodi Picoult, The Popcorn Board, Barbara Prest, Susan G. Purdy, Beth Stevens, Trisha Thompson, Emily B. Todd, Penny Warner, Tracey Watson, Stacey Webb, and Helen Wolt.

We extend our gratitude to *FamilyFun*'s many creative readers who shared with us the recipes and tips that have been a success with their own families. Thanks to Bonnie Alexander, Kim Arant, the Aydinel family, Julie Banal, Rebecca Bean, Martha Browning, Laura Burnes, Christine Calderiao, Julie Carlisle, Paula Chabot, Doris Creter, Lonnie Davis, Robert Davis, Terry Doyle, the Duggar family, Julie Dunlap, Ryan Elder, Karyn Everham, Michelle Fehlman, Victoria Franzese, Susan Freeman, Ruth Gill, Ella Graney, Brook Hampton, Roberta Henderson, Jill Hibbard, Vicki Hodges, Rhonda Huguet, Cathy Hunter, Tina Katz, Julie Jones, Cady Kilpeck, Shelley Kotulka, Kimberly Kroener, Jeanine Manser, Dee Martin, Amy Nappa, Deanne Nutaitis, Mary Patten, Candace Pease, Melissa Rowan, Liz Ruff, Meg Ryan, Heather Sciford, Susan Schumaker, Rivana Stadtlander, Christy Turner, Monica Uhe, David and Birdie Lynn Vining, Stephanie Weight, and the Wingfield family.

This book would not have been possible without the talented *FamilyFun* magazine staff, who edited and art-directed the recipes for previous versions of the magazine. In addition to the book staff credited on the previous page, we'd like to acknowledge the following staff members: Jonathan Adolph, Doug Bantz, Nicole Blasenak, Kristen Branch, Jodi Butler, Terry Carr, Jean Cranston, Naomi Adler Dancis, Barbara Findlen, Isadora Fox, Mary Giles, Moira Greto, Michael Grinley, Ginger Barr Heafey, Beth Honeyman, Debra Immergut, Elaine Kehoe, Kandy Littrell, Laura MacKay, Mark Mantegna, Samuel Mead, Adrienne Stolarz, Mike Trotman, Ellen Harter Wall, and Sandra L. Wickland.

We also would like to thank our partners at Disney Editions, especially Wendy Lefkon and Jessica Ward.

Special thanks to all the photographers, stylists, and models for their excellent work, which first appeared in *FamilyFun* magazine.

STYLISTS

Bonnie Anderson, Kim Brent, Carol Cole, Bettina Fisher, Susan Fox, Helen Jones, Lee Levine, Anne Lewis, Janet Miller, Marie Piraino, Karen Quatsoe, Edwina Stevenson, Laura Torres, Lynn Zimmerman

PHOTOGRAPHERS

Reena Bammi: 117 (top four), 124, 125, 148, 149, 213 (left two), 216, 217 Paul Berg: 49, 50, 51, 128 (bottom), 129, 133, 172, 174, 175, 178, 181 (top), 215 Peter N. Fox: 29, 205 (bottom) Andrew Greto: 12 (bottom right), 13 (top right), 157 John Gruen: front cover, 6 (top), 10, 11, 14, 20 (bottom), 22, 23, 33 (top), 34, 35, 38, 58, 59, 64, 65, 86, 100, 101, 104, 105, 106, 108, 110, 111, 112, 119 (bottom two), 122, 123, 126, 138, 139, 147, 162, 163, 166, 176, 177, 186, 196, 197 (bottom), 206, 207, 210, 211, back cover (left) Jacqueline Hopkins: 6 (bottom), 9, 20 (top left), 21, 24, 33 (bottom), 60, 85 (bottom), 92, 94, 96, 103, 109, 113, 115, 173 Ed Judice: 26, 27, 36, 37, 44 (top left), 47, 68, 71 (right middle), 79 (bottom), 81 (bottom), 82, 83, 85 (top), 88, 90, 128 (top left), 137 (bottom), 160, 171, 194, 200, 202, 208 Lightworks Photographic: 53 Mark Mantegna: 7 (top), 17 (bottom), 79 (top), 81 (top) Joanne Schmaltz: 6 (middle), 7(bottom three), 12 (top left), 17 (top), 18, 28, 32, 40, 42 (bottom), 43 (top), 45, 46, 52, 55 (top), 56, 57, 62, 66, 67 (top), 69, 72, 74, 77, 78, 80, 84, 89, 98, 114, 118, 119 (top), 121, 130, 131 (top), 132, 136, 137 (top), 140, 141, 143, 144, 145, 146, 151, 152 (top), 153, 155, 156, 158, 159, 161, 165, 169, 170, 182, 184, 185, 190, 193, 199, 201, 203, 204, 205 (top), 209, 212, 214 Shaffer/Smith Photography: 16, 19, 25, 30, 31, 41, 42 (top), 43 (bottom right), 44 (middle and bottom), 48, 54, 55 (bottom), 63, 67 (bottom), 70, 73, 75, 76, 91, 97, 116, 117 (bottom), 120, 131 (bottom), 134, 168, 180, 181 (bottom), 183, 189, 191, 192, 195, 197 (top), 198, 213 (far right), 218, 219, 223, back cover (right), spine Becky Luigart-Stayner: 188 Edwina Stevenson: 13 (middle), 71 (top and bottom), 152 (bottom), 164 Katie Winger: illustrations, 113

PAGE 22

PAGE 40

PAGE 84

Contents

PAGE 81

PAGE 118

PAGE 150

PAGE 208

Let's Cook Together

As a busy mom of two busy girls, I've learned that sometimes the best place to spend time together is in our kitchen. While I'm trying to get lunches made for school or put dinner on the table, I often give Ella, 9, and Maisie, 6, the role of kitchen helpers — washing lettuce in the salad spinner or cutting tomatoes with a plastic knife. As we cook, the girls not only learn their way around the kitchen, they also open up and tell me stories about their day, like who they played with at recess, and why they absolutely have to get their ears pierced.

For me, finding recipes that we can cook together is the easy part. As one of the editors of this book, I'm fortunate to have a lot of amazing recipes from *FamilyFun* magazine at my fingertips.

When choosing recipes to print, we always look for foods that will please adults like us and our children (well, most of them anyway). Every *FamilyFun* recipe then has to pass the approval of our test kitchen to ensure that the steps are kid-friendly and the ingredients are easy to find. Lucky for us, we get to help with the taste-testing, sampling delicious foods like the Wonderful Waffles on page 26, the Homemade Ranch Dip for fresh veggies on page 73, and the Blueberry Pie on page 212.

That's why we feel so certain that when you and your kids step into the kitchen, you'll be delighted with what you create. Hopefully, you'll also learn a thing or two about your children's day.

— *Deanna Cook*

P.S. My daughter Ella's favorite recipe is the Peanut Butter Noodles on page 161; Maisie's favorite is the World's Simplest Bread dough on page 116, which she loves to shape into teddy bears and turtles. What recipes in this book are your kids' favorites? Email us at CookingKids.FamilyFun @Disney.com.

SETTING UP A KID-FRIENDLY KITCHEN

Around my house — and yours too, I suspect — the kitchen beats the living room hands down for actual living. So how can we make the kitchen accessible to even the youngest chefs in the family? Here are some tried-and-true tips.

CREATE A SPACE FOR LITTLE COOKS: Set up a low table with two chairs in a corner of your kitchen. If you don't have space for this, use an island or a pull-out shelf. Invest in a sturdy step stool and store it in a place where kids can get to it easily.

STOCK UP ON KID-SIZE KITCHEN TOOLS: Providing a selection of kid-size tools is an inviting way to say "Wanna help?" Reserve a drawer in the kitchen and stock it with a mini rolling pin, whisk, baking sheet, plastic picnic knives, an apron, and cookie cutters. Alternatively, you can designate a lower cabinet just for kid storage. That way, they can help themselves to cooking tools as well as plastic cups, bowls, and other items they are likely to need.

ENCOURAGE CLEANUP: Pint-size sponges or a toy broom and dustpan hung within a kid's reach lets children experience the satisfaction of pitching in.

WRITE YOUR OWN KIDS' COOKBOOK: Start a recipe file specifically for chefs in training. You can either write the individual recipes on index cards and store them in a plastic case, or jot down the recipes on paper and store them in a loose-leaf binder. Don't forget to let your children decorate the book or box cover with their names. Once your kids start collecting their favorite recipes, they'll chip in more with dinner planning and preparation.

KITCHEN CRAFT
Dish Towel Apron

· · · · · · · · · · · · · · · · · · · ·

Your kitchen helper will feel proud when he puts on this apron at the start of each kitchen task.

1 Fold over the top corners of a cotton, terry, or linen dish towel and press the creases flat with a hot iron.

2 Create sleeves for the ribbon by making evenly spaced stitches across each corner flap, parallel to the folded edge and about ½ inch from it.

3 Thread about 2 yards of ½- to ¾-inch-wide ribbon up through one sleeve, then down through the other. Leave a loop at the top for your child's head and long strings hanging from both sides. Knot the ends of the ribbon so they won't pull through the sleeves.

4 To shorten the apron — and to add a useful pocket — fold up the bottom of the dish towel to the desired length, then iron it flat. Stitch the edges in place and, if you like, sew 2 lines down the front to create compartments.

MY GREAT IDEA
Lights, Camera, Cooking!

When it comes to cooking with kids, sometimes a small project can become a big production. Several families told us they host their own pretend cooking shows as a way to get their kids excited about cooking. When Tina Katz started a Mamma and Me Cooking Show in her Brooklyn, New York, kitchen, she had no idea what an impact it would have on her six-year-old daughter's eating habits. Her daughter not only plays chef during her "show," she also teaches her imaginary audience about the benefits of healthy eating.

COOKING WITH KIDS

Teaching your kids to cook adds up to a lot more than showing them how groceries become dinner. Through cooking, they can learn nutrition, organization, math, and science. Take full advantage of this time together in the kitchen by being prepared. Here are a few tips to get you started.

START YOUNG: Invite the kids into the kitchen early so they get accustomed to the variety of sights, sounds, and smells. With babies, you can put them in the backpack to watch you cook. With toddlers, give them small projects to do — rinse asparagus in their toy kitchen, tear lettuce into pieces, sprinkle grated cheese on pasta, or crush graham cracker crumbs in a ziplock bag.

INVOLVE YOUR CHILD IN YOUR COOKING PROJECTS: Whether you're making dinner or packing school lunch, let the kids do small parts of whatever you're doing. They can cut green peppers to add to a pot of soup, rinse canned black beans in a colander for chili, and slice bananas for a fruit salad. Stuck on what jobs to give them? Look for our "Kids' Steps" within each recipe.

If your kids help make the meal, they will likely be more inclined to eat it.

LET KIDS PLAY WITH THEIR FOOD: Encourage your kids to have fun with ingredients — to feel the texture of a pile of flour, smell the spices before they're added to the soup pot, and turn their vegetables into playful faces. This will help make new foods more familiar.

MIX IN SOME LEARNING: From colors and numbers to fractions and basic chemistry, cooking offers fun, hands-on opportunities for learning.

FOCUS ON THE PROCESS, NOT THE END PRODUCT: Kids love cooking. Even if their food turns out slightly lopsided, they feel proud. So relax, forget about the mess, and have fun together.

KITCHEN AIDS
Tools of the Trade

Give your child implements that really work, and you'll be amazed by how well she can help (with supervision, of course). Some of our safe yet functional favorites:

POTATO MASHER for smashing cooked apples for applesauce, bananas for banana bread, and, of course, cooked potatoes.

UNBREAKABLE JAR with a screw-on lid, for shaking up salad dressing.

SALAD SPINNER to dry lettuce and other leafy greens. The push-top kind, as shown, is the easiest for children to manipulate.

BABY FOOD MILL for safe, fuss-free pureeing of cooked fruits and veggies. Even your preschooler can grind up first meals for a new sibling.

KIDS' SCISSORS to cut up fresh basil, dill, or parsley for soups and salads. Just be sure the scissors are clean!

PLASTIC PICNIC KNIFE to cut up soft vegetables, such as mushrooms and cherry tomatoes, as well as cheese and other easy-to-cut foods. As they gain skill and age, kids can advance to a paring knife.

TEACHING TIPS
Kids' Cooking 101

◆ Teach kids good cooking habits from the get-go. For example: wash hands, wear an apron, tie hair back, never touch a hot stove, and always help clean up.

◆ Read the recipe through with your kids and make sure everyone understands it. Teach kids that following directions carefully yields the best results.

◆ Have kids collect and set out all the ingredients on a tray. As you use each item, have the kids wrap and put away the remainder.

◆ Be sure to teach kids how to handle equipment and knives safely. Let young kids start with a plastic picnic knife, then graduate to a paring knife. Monitor their proficiency as you work together.

◆ Teach kids how to measure carefully and accurately. They should spoon, not scoop, flour and confectioners' sugar into dry measuring cups, and level these ingredients gently with a knife. For liquids, use glass or plastic cups with a pouring spout. Show them how to read the measurements at eye level.

PLANNING HEALTHY MEALS

Kids can often be reluctant to try new food — especially if they've been told it's good for them. One way to demystify a new dish is to get your kids involved in its creation, from making the meal plan to buying the ingredients to helping with the cooking.

INVOLVE THE KIDS IN THE MEAL PLANNING: At the beginning of the week, make a menu plan with your kids. Talk about what makes a balanced menu, then have each child (and parent) pick a healthy meal for one night. You can ask your kids to be the guest chef on their night (with your help, of course).

LET THE KIDS HELP WITH THE SHOPPING: At the store, have your kids explore the produce aisle and pick out a new fruit or veggie to buy. If they've picked it, they're more likely to try it.

TEACH KIDS WHERE FOOD COMES FROM: Some kids may not know that carrots have tops or that zucchini has blossoms. To take the mystery out of food, visit your local market, grow vegetables in your backyard, or take a tour of your bakery or pizza parlor.

SERVE VEGGIES RAW OR FROZEN: If your kids like frozen peas, why fight it? Lots of parents have told us that icy peas please. Likewise, many kids prefer raw veggies over baked or boiled.

SKIP THE FORKS: The Hendersons of Lawrenceville, Georgia, enjoy "Fun Utensil Night," says mom Roberta. "We put a variety of utensils on the table, and everyone gets to pick one or two to eat their veggies with. Some favorites are spatulas, ice cream scoops, drink umbrellas, and tongs."

REMEMBER THAT LOOKS MATTER: Offer young children visually appealing choices: fresh fruit arranged in a silly face, or peppers cut into hearts or stars with cookie cutters. Try mini veggies. Victoria Franzese, a mother of two from New York City, says, "Mini corn and grape tomatoes are cute; baby carrots always win against the large sort."

TRY NEW RECIPES: Children are notoriously unadventurous eaters, but keep in mind that most tastes are acquired. Try something new at dinner, and if the kids don't like it, reintroduce it a month later.

DINNER TABLE FUN

If life often feels like a storm of obligations — car pools for soccer games, housework, homework — the family dinner table can be a kind of life raft. It's a safe place to gather with the people we love, enjoy good food, and catch up on the events of the day. Families being families, however, suppertime can also be as relaxed as a catered hurricane. If your own dinners have been a little stormy lately, try these ideas.

MAKE MEALS FUN: *FamilyFun* reader Karyn Everham and her husband made mealtimes more fun (and predictable for their picky boys) by having a theme assigned to each day. Whether it's Seafood Sunday, Mexican Monday, or One Pot Wednesday, the family all get involved in planning the menu. Karyn says, "Thanks to theme nights, supper isn't the chore it used to be. And, it's brought us closer as a family."

SET A NICE TABLE: It takes only moments to throw a pretty cloth over the table and light a candle or two, but these simple details can make dinner feel like a grand occasion — even if the menu is as simple as burgers and hot dogs.

STAY ON TOP OF TABLE MANNERS: At the Rowans' in Mountain Home, Idaho, the child who exhibits the best manners gets to blow out the candle at the end of the meal. The Huguet family of Missoula, Montana, passes out ten pennies to each person at the beginning of the meal, and if the kids slurp or burp at the table, they have to pay a penny.

KEEP THE CONVERSATION ROLLING: Around the dinner table in the Doyle house in Springfield, Pennsylvania, everyone takes a turn telling the best and worst thing about their day. Mom Susan Schumaker of Overland Park, Kansas, uses a Native American practice, the talking stick, to prevent conversation free-for-alls. Only the person holding the stick (actually a flower or other handy item)

can speak. When they're done, they pass the item to the next speaker. Not only do occupied kids eat better (and stay at the table longer), sharing thoughts and feelings brings everyone closer — and that's what family meals are all about.

CELEBRATE AT THE TABLE: Celebrate holidays such as Chinese New Year, Cinco de Mayo, and Columbus Day by serving foods from related countries (in this case, China, Mexico, and Italy). Or, celebrate little things, like a good report card, a winning soccer season, or a job promotion.

Napkin Origami

Make your dinner table feel like a fancy restaurant with the following easy napkin fold for cloth or paper napkins.

THE POCKET FOLD

1 Start with a square cloth or paper napkin (unfolded) and place the outside facedown. Fold down the upper left-hand corner to the center of the napkin.

2 Fold up the bottom half to form a rectangle.

3 Fold over the left side to form a square.

4 Flip the square over.

5 Fold the right side over the left and fill the pocket with utensils as shown above.

CHAPTER ONE

BREAKFAST

Wake up with some delicious, eye-opening recipes

FOR MANY FAMILIES, SUNDAY BREAKFAST is the best meal of the week. We get to stay in our pajamas and flip stacks of pancakes or bake warm scones or muffins. But school-day breakfasts share little of that charm. The morning rush hour often leaves us nagging our kids to hurry up and eat so they don't miss the bus. So, how do you turn breakfast into a favorite meal — or at least a pleasant one — every day of the week? You can start with these simple tips.

SET UP A CEREAL STATION. Let your kids grab their own breakfast on busy mornings from a self-service area — a low cupboard with boxes of cereal, bowls, and spoons. Keep small pitchers of milk and orange juice on a low shelf in the fridge too.

PUT A TIMER IN CHARGE. If your kids are dawdlers, take a tip from *FamilyFun* reader Julie Carlisle of Pompano Beach, Florida, and set a timer for 15 minutes. She used to spend her mornings saying "Eat! Eat!" but now she tells her kids that when the timer rings, breakfast is over.

BOOK IT. If bickering children slow down your breakfast, encourage them to read while they eat — or read to them — for a happy distraction.

CREATE A PEACEFUL MOMENT. On weekday mornings, the Chabot children of Rockland, Massachusetts, sometimes enjoy a simple breakfast in bed. While they eat, Mom and Dad get dressed and ready for work, and the whole family chats. The tradition "helps us spend some peaceful time together before the rush," says mom Paula.

ON WEEKENDS, COOK FROM SCRATCH. After a bustling week at school and work, a leisurely weekend morning is a great time to teach your kids how to cook omelets, flip crepes, or bake muffins. You might designate Saturday as Try a New Recipe Day or make a weekly tradition of favorites like homemade waffles.

Favorite Omelet Fillings

Just what fillings make the best omelet is really a matter of personal taste. So encourage your child to have fun and experiment with different combinations of her favorite vegetables, cheeses, meats, and herbs. Here are a few suggestions we think are particularly flavorful.

◆ Steamed broccoli, grated Cheddar cheese, and chopped cooked ham

◆ Fresh chopped herbs (such as chives, basil, or parsley) and cottage cheese

◆ Diced cooked chicken or turkey with diced green or red pepper

◆ Refried beans topped with salsa and Monterey Jack cheese

◆ Crisp bacon bits and shredded Cheddar cheese

◆ Sautéed mushrooms and chopped spinach

PREP TIME: 5 minutes **COOKING TIME:** about 5 minutes

Easy Omelets

A leisurely weekend morning is a great time to teach your child the art of filling and folding a breakfast omelet.

INGREDIENTS
- 2 eggs
- 1 teaspoon water
-    Pinch of salt
- 1 tablespoon butter
- ½ cup omelet filling (see left)

1 Crack the eggs into a small bowl. Add the water and salt and use a fork to beat the mixture just until blended.

2 Heat your frying pan on medium-high. Add the butter and spread it over the entire bottom of the pan as it melts.

3 Pour the beaten eggs into the pan and cook the omelet, following the step-by-step directions below. Serves 1.

KIDS' STEPS Older kids can crack the eggs and flip the omelet. Younger kids can beat the eggs.

TEACHING KIDS TO COOK
How to Cook an Omelet

Wait for the bottom of the eggs to cook a little, then gently push the eggs away from the edge. Tilt the pan so the uncooked egg runs into the spot you've created.

When the omelet surface looks almost cooked, add the filling over half of it. Slide a spatula under the plain half and fold it over the filling. The eggs should now be fully cooked.

To serve, tilt up the pan handle and slide the omelet out of the pan and onto your plate.

Mini Frittatas

For a fun and easy morning meal, try these small-scale egg dishes. Baked in individual muffin cups, they ensure that everyone gets the mix-ins they like.

INGREDIENTS

- 4 eggs
- ¼ cup half-and-half
- ½ teaspoon salt
- Assorted mix-ins, such as shredded cheese, diced vegetables, and cooked and chopped bacon, ham, or sausage
- Grated Parmesan cheese (optional)

1 Heat your oven to 350° and coat a 6-cup muffin pan with nonstick cooking spray.

2 Whisk together the eggs, half-and-half, and salt in a medium bowl, then evenly distribute the egg mixture among the muffin cups.

3 Add about 2 tablespoons of mix-ins to each cup, then sprinkle on a bit of Parmesan cheese, if you like.

4 Bake the frittatas until they are puffy and the edges are golden brown, about 20 to 25 minutes. Makes 6 mini frittatas.

KIDS' STEPS Kids can beat the eggs, prepare the mix-ins, and add them to the cups.

QUICK TRICK
Breakfast Burritos

On the morning after a Mexican dinner, you can use your leftovers as filling for a delicious roll-up breakfast sandwich.

1   tablespoon butter
6   eggs, beaten
5   8-inch flour tortillas

FILLING OPTIONS

1/2   cup grated Monterey Jack cheese
1   plum tomato, chopped
1   small onion, diced
1/4   green or red pepper, chopped
1/2   avocado, diced
    Salsa
    Black olives, sliced

Over medium-high heat, melt the butter in a frying pan and scramble and cook the eggs to your liking.

    Meanwhile, warm the tortillas for a few minutes on the rack of a 250° oven, then fill with the scrambled egg and your choice of fillings. Roll into a burrito. Serves 5.

PREP TIME: about 25 minutes   BAKING TIME: about 35 minutes

Royal Ham and Eggs

This baked dish is perfect for weekend guests or a holiday brunch.

INGREDIENTS

1   loaf of French bread, cut into 1/2-inch cubes
1/2   pound cooked ham or sausage, cubed
1   8-ounce package frozen chopped spinach, thawed and drained
12   cherry tomatoes, sliced in half
8   ounces Cheddar cheese, grated
8   eggs
1   teaspoon dried mustard
1/4   teaspoon pepper
1   cup milk

1 Heat the oven to 350°. Butter a 13- by 9- by 2-inch baking dish and line with the bread cubes.

2 Cover the bread with layers of ham or sausage, chopped spinach, cherry tomatoes, and grated cheese.

3 In a separate bowl, whisk the eggs, dried mustard, pepper, and milk. Pour the mixture over the casserole.

4 Bake for 30 minutes, then broil for 2 minutes or until the cheese turns golden brown. Makes 8 to 10 servings.

KIDS' STEPS Kids can measure the ingredients, beat the eggs, and layer the casserole.

18 EGGS

Egg in a Nest

Instead of serving your egg on toast, try serving it *in* toast. This breakfast classic is also known as Egg in a Saddle, Egyptian Egg, and One Eye.

INGREDIENTS

- 1 egg
- 1 slice of bread
- 1 tablespoon butter

1 Crack the egg into a bowl and set the bowl aside.

2 Use a 3-inch cookie cutter (circle, heart, star, or flower) to cut a shape out of the piece of bread.

3 Melt the butter in a frying pan over medium heat. Place the bread in the pan and fry it lightly on one side (you can also fry the cutout shape). Flip the bread over. Reduce the heat to low.

4 Carefully pour the egg into the cutout hole in the middle of the bread. Cover the pan and cook for 2 to 3 minutes or until the egg has set in the bread "nest." For an over-easy egg, flip the egg and bread and cook it on the other side. Serves 1.

 KIDS' STEPS Kids can crack the egg, use a cookie cutter, and flip the egg.

TIP: When pouring the egg into the nest, remind your child not to touch the side of the hot pan (this is a job for adults and kids ages 8 and up).

COOKING BASICS
Well-Timed Eggs

SOFT-BOILED EGGS: In a saucepan, cover whole eggs with water and bring to a boil. Reduce the heat to a simmer and cook for 2 to 3 minutes more. Remove the eggs from the pan and plunge them into cold water to halt the cooking and make peeling the shell easier.

HARD-BOILED EGGS: In a saucepan, cover whole eggs with water and bring to a boil. Remove the pan from the heat and leave the eggs in the hot water for 15 minutes more. Plunge the eggs into cold water to halt the cooking and make peeling the shell easier.

NOTE: Add 2 minutes to cooking times if the eggs are straight from the refrigerator.

Buttermilk Pancakes

Simple to prepare and fun to customize, this recipe may inspire young chefs to start a weekend tradition.

INGREDIENTS

- 2   cups flour
- 2   teaspoons baking soda
- 1/2   teaspoon salt
- 2   tablespoons sugar
- 2   eggs
- 2   cups buttermilk (to substitute, add 1 tablespoon of lemon juice or white vinegar to 2 cups of milk and let stand for 10 minutes)
- 3   tablespoons vegetable oil
-     Butter for the pan
- 1   cup fruit, such as blueberries or raspberries, or apple or banana slices (optional)

1 Sift the flour, baking soda, salt, and sugar into a large bowl.

2 Beat the eggs and buttermilk in a separate bowl, then beat in the oil. Pour the egg mixture over the dry ingredients and stir, but do not beat. The batter will be a little bit lumpy, but that's okay.

3 Melt 1 tablespoon of the butter in a frying pan on medium-high. Then, being careful not to splatter the hot butter, drop about 1/4 cup of batter for each pancake into the pan. Be sure to leave enough room between the cakes for them to grow. If you are adding fruit pieces, gently press them into the batter.

4 Cook the pancakes until the bubbles that form on the top burst. Then, flip and cook the other side until golden brown. Makes 15 to 20 pancakes.

 Kids can measure and sift the dry ingredients, beat the eggs, and stir the batter.

FUN FOOD
Personalized Pancakes

· · · · · · · · · · · · · · · ·

For fun, you can drizzle pancake batter into shapes. Just pour the batter into a plastic bag, snip a small hole in one corner, and squeeze the mix into hearts, teddy bears, numbers, or your child's initials on the hot griddle.

TEACHING KIDS TO COOK
Pancake Pointers

THE BATTER: It should flow thickly from your ladle, but not so thickly that it falls in lumps. If it needs thinning, stir in 2 tablespoons of milk.

THE FLIP: Wait too long and your pancakes will be dry and rubbery. Flip too soon and they'll be pale and undercooked. The time to flip is when you notice these 3 things simultaneously: 1. The little air bubbles that have appeared on the surface begin to burst. 2. The perimeter of the pancake looks a bit dry. 3. The underside is golden brown.

THE COOKING SURFACE: A heavy cast-iron skillet is ideal because it heats evenly and gives pancakes a slightly crisp, golden brown surface. Nonstick skillets are good too, but the dark coating sometimes browns pancakes too deeply. If that happens, turn the heat down a little. Electric griddles are convenient because you can preset the temperature and cook up to 6 pancakes at a time.

THE TECHNIQUE: Don't poke or press down on the pancake. Allow it to cook undisturbed until it's ready to flip. It is okay, however, to lift the edge to check the browning underneath.

Oatmeal Pancakes

These flapjacks are comforting and filling. Try adding chopped nuts or dried fruit for a special treat.

INGREDIENTS

- 2   eggs
- 2   tablespoons vegetable oil
- 1   cup all-purpose flour, or ½ cup all-purpose and ½ cup whole wheat
- 1   cup rolled oats
- 1½ teaspoons baking powder
- ½   teaspoon salt
- ¾   cup orange juice (preferably fresh)
- 2   tablespoons butter
- ½   cup chopped nuts or dried fruit (optional)

1 Mix the eggs with the oil. Separately, combine the flour, oats, baking powder, and salt in a medium bowl.

2 Stir the egg mixture into the dry ingredients, then stir in the orange juice.

3 Heat the butter in a large frying pan, then drop about ¼ cup of batter for each pancake into the pan. Sprinkle on nuts or fruit, if desired. Cook one side until the bubbles that form on the top burst. Then flip and cook until the other sides are golden brown. Makes 6 pancakes.

KIDS' STEPS   Younger kids can measure and mix the ingredients. Older kids can flip the flapjacks.

COOKING BASICS
Whole Grain Pancake Mix

Preparing this mix will take you and your child just a few minutes, but you'll enjoy leisurely breakfasts for weeks.

- 5   cups all-purpose flour
- 1½   cups whole wheat flour
- 1   cup cornmeal
- ⅓   cup sugar
- 2   tablespoons plus 2 teaspoons baking powder
- 2   teaspoons salt

Measure the all-purpose flour, whole wheat flour, cornmeal, sugar, baking powder, and salt into a large bowl of a food processor and combine. Spoon the mix into a 2-quart jar.

To give the jar a professional look in your pantry, have your child affix a label on the front that reads "Pancake Mix" and a second label on the back with the pancake directions: "Stir 1½ cups of pancake mix, 2 eggs, and 1¼ cups of milk in a mixing bowl until smooth. Melt 1 tablespoon of butter in a large frying pan over medium heat. Cook the pancakes for 2 to 3 minutes on each side. Enjoy with maple syrup. Serves 4."

PREP TIME: **10** minutes   COOKING TIME: **about 5 minutes per pancake**

Blueberry Pancakes

Take advantage of blueberry season by making this delectable fruit-filled breakfast.

INGREDIENTS

1 3/4	cups flour
2	tablespoons sugar
1	teaspoon baking powder
1/2	teaspoon baking soda
1/2	teaspoon salt
1/4	teaspoon nutmeg
2	eggs
1	cup milk
1	cup sour cream
1/4	cup melted butter or vegetable oil, plus extra for the pan
1/2	teaspoon vanilla extract
1/2	teaspoon finely grated lemon zest
1 1/2	cups fresh blueberries

1 Sift the flour, sugar, baking powder, baking soda, salt, and nutmeg into a large mixing bowl.

2 In a separate large bowl, lightly whisk the eggs. Add the milk, sour cream, melted butter (or oil), and vanilla extract and whisk to blend.

3 Make a well in the dry ingredients and pour the liquid mixture into it. Vigorously whisk the ingredients just until blended (about 10 seconds).

KIDS' STEPS Younger kids can sift the dry ingredients into the bowl. Older kids can ladle the batter into the pan and flip the pancakes.

4 Add the lemon zest and the blueberries and gently fold them into the batter with a rubber spatula.

5 Heat a large frying pan or skillet over medium heat for 3 to 4 minutes. Then pour in enough butter to coat the surface. Using a pot holder to grasp the pan handle with both hands, gently swirl the skillet around to evenly distribute the butter.

6 For each pancake, ladle about 1/4 cup of batter onto the hot skillet.

7 Cook the pancakes on one side until the bubbles that form on top burst. Then flip and cook until the bottoms are golden brown.

8 Serve the pancakes at once, preferably on warm plates. Top with butter and maple syrup. Makes about 15 pancakes.

French Toast

The best French toast is made from the densest bread. Challah is our first choice, then brioche or sourdough. If all else fails, a premium sandwich bread can stand up to the task.

INGREDIENTS

   4   eggs
  ½   cup milk
   1   teaspoon vanilla extract
   2   tablespoons butter or oil, for pan
   8   slices dense bread

1 In a shallow bowl or pie plate, beat the eggs, then mix in the milk and vanilla extract. Heat the butter in a frying pan over medium heat.

2 Soak the slices of bread in the egg mixture, turning once. They should be saturated but not falling apart.

3 Brown the bread in the skillet, turning once, about 2 to 3 minutes on each side. Serves 4.

KIDS' STEPS   Kids can crack the eggs into the bowl and dip the bread in the egg mixture.

MAPLE FRENCH TOAST: Brown both sides of the French toast, then sprinkle grated maple sugar candy on the top and turn. Cook for 1 minute. Sprinkle the other side and turn once more.

BANANA FRENCH TOAST: Cut a pocket in the top crust of a 1½-inch slice of Italian bread and stuff with a few banana slices. Dip in the egg mixture and cook as directed in step 3.

PREP TIME: **10 minutes**   COOKING TIME: **about 2 minutes per crepe**

Classic Crepes

With this recipe, your aspiring young chef can get the skinny on those thin pancakes that are a staple of French cuisine.

INGREDIENTS

- 3   eggs
- 1½   cups milk
- 1   cup plus 2 tablespoons flour
- 1   tablespoon sugar (1 teaspoon for dinner crepes)
- ¼   teaspoon salt
- 2   tablespoons melted butter

1 Put all the ingredients in a blender in the order listed and blend until smooth. Remove the lid and scrape down the sides with a rubber spatula. Briefly blend the mixture again. Set the covered blender in the refrigerator for 30 minutes or even overnight.

KIDS' STEPS Younger kids can measure ingredients and press the buttons on the blender. Older kids can pour the batter into the skillet and flip the crepes.

2 When it's time to cook the crepes, use a paper towel to spread about 1 teaspoon of butter or vegetable oil in the bottom of an 8- or 9-inch shallow nonstick frying pan and place over medium heat. Blend the batter again to smooth it.

3 For the first crepe, pour ¼ to ⅓ cup of batter into a measuring cup to gauge how much to use. For the rest of the crepes, pour approximately that much batter right from the blender. Cook each crepe, following the steps below. Adjust the heat if they brown too quickly or too slowly. Makes 12 crepes.

ADD-INS
Crepe Fillings
. . . .

Besides being quick to cook and fun to flip, crepes are versatile enough to serve for breakfast, dinner, or even dessert, depending on what you fill them with. Some sweet fillings are:

◆ Jam and cream cheese mixed with a bit of vanilla extract
◆ Mini chocolate chips and banana slices
◆ Sliced peaches and honey
◆ Nutella and ice cream

TEACHING KIDS TO COOK
How to Make a Crepe

Pour the batter into your heated pan, well to one side. Immediately tilt and swirl the pan to evenly coat the bottom. This should take about 5 seconds.

Cook the crepe on the first side for about 45 seconds, then quickly flip it with a spatula and cook the other side for about half as long.

Grasping the pan securely, swiftly invert it so the cooked crepe will fall onto a large plate. Rub a little butter in the pan before cooking the next crepe.

PREP TIME: 10 minutes   **COOKING TIME:** about 4 minutes per waffle

Wonderful Waffles

INGREDIENTS

2 eggs

1 2/3 cups milk

1/3 cup vegetable oil

2 cups flour

1 tablespoon baking powder

2 tablespoons sugar

1/2 teaspoon salt

Cooking spray

This no-frills batter is quick and easy to prepare, and it's just right for young kids learning to follow a recipe. Once they've mastered the basics, they can try turning their waffles into art (see opposite page).

1 Set up the waffle iron on a tabletop at your child's level. Plug the iron in and remind him to be careful when working around it.

2 Next, crack the eggs into a large bowl and whisk until frothy. Add the milk and vegetable oil, then mix. In a separate bowl, measure the flour, baking powder, sugar, and salt, then stir.

3 Add the dry ingredients to the milk mixture and stir until the lumps disappear.

4 Spray the preheated waffle iron on both sides with cooking spray. If you are using a nonstick waffle iron or if your waffle iron is well seasoned, you may be able to skip this step.

5 Show your child how to carefully pour the batter onto the center of the iron. Close the lid.

6 Bake until the waffles are cooked through, about 2 to 4 minutes. You'll know they are done when the waffle iron stops steaming. Makes 5 waffles.

KIDS' STEPS Younger kids can stir the waffle mix. Older kids can pour the batter.

Waffle Art

Your family can have fun adding a fruity flair to this breakfast favorite. Cook round waffles (homemade or store-bought) then adorn them with berries and sliced or chopped fruits to create tasty designs. Here are three that will inspire your kids.

INGREDIENTS

Round waffles

Assorted fruit, such as bananas, kiwis, strawberries, apples, raspberries, pears, and blueberries

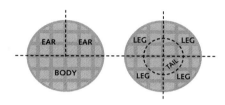

FLOWER (1 waffle): Arrange slices of pear, skin side up, below a waffle for a flower stem and leaves, as shown. Then, decorate the waffle flower center with berries and arrange apple slice petals around it.

BUTTERFLY (2 waffles): Cut both waffles in half and arrange the pieces around a banana for the insect's body, as shown. Add kiwi antennae and decorate the wings with slices of kiwi, strawberry, and banana.

DOG (3 waffles): Set 1 whole waffle in place for the dog's head. Cut the 2 remaining waffles (see diagram), then arrange the pieces as shown. Add a blueberry nose and eyes, a slice of apple for a collar, and a strawberry slice for a tongue.

FUN FOOD

Birthday Pancakes

• •

Celebrate your child's big day right from the get-go with a stack of birthday pancakes. To make the treat extra sweet, drizzle her hotcakes with maple syrup, chocolate sauce, fruit, or whipped cream. Top it off with candles.

KIDS' STEPS Kids can cut the waffles into different shapes and make designs with the fruit pieces.

Quick-Mix Bran Muffins

A box of cereal becomes a warm and hearty breakfast with this simple muffin recipe that can be whipped up in a snap.

INGREDIENTS

2 1/2   cups flour
1   cup sugar
1   teaspoon baking soda
1   teaspoon salt
2   eggs, beaten
2   cups buttermilk
1/2   cup vegetable oil
3 1/2   cups raisin-and-bran cereal

1 In a large mixing bowl, combine the flour, sugar, baking soda, and salt. Add the eggs, buttermilk, and oil, stirring just until there are no traces of flour. Fold in the cereal.

2 Heat the oven to 400°. Grease a 12-cup and 6-cup muffin pan (or line them with paper bake cups) and fill them with batter. Bake until done, about 15 to 20 minutes. Makes 18.

KIDS' STEPS Kids can line the muffin pans with paper cups and measure and mix the muffin ingredients.

Carrot Muffins

This moist carrot muffin has the added nutrition of pineapple and applesauce. Each one supplies almost half of your child's daily requirement of vitamin A.

INGREDIENTS

1   cup (8-ounce can) crushed pineapple in its own juice
3   cups flour
2   cups sugar
1   teaspoon baking soda
1   teaspoon baking powder
1   teaspoon salt
2   teaspoons cinnamon
2   eggs
1   egg white
1/2   cup vegetable oil
2   teaspoons vanilla extract
2   cups coarsely shredded carrots
1/2   cup applesauce

1 Heat the oven to 350°. Drain the pineapple and reserve the juice. In a large bowl, whisk together the flour, sugar, baking soda, baking powder, salt, and cinnamon.

2 Make a well in the center of the mixture and drop in the eggs, egg white, oil, vanilla extract, and reserved pineapple juice. Beat at medium speed until blended, about 1 1/2 minutes. With a spoon, stir in the crushed pineapple, shredded carrots, and applesauce.

3 Grease the cups of two 12-muffin bake pans (or line them with paper bake cups) and fill them with batter, using an ice-cream scoop, if you like. Bake until a toothpick stuck in the center of a muffin comes out clean, about 20 minutes. Remove the pans from the oven and cool on a wire rack for 2 minutes. Serve warm. Makes 24.

KIDS' STEPS Kids can separate the egg, fold in the fruit, and fill the muffin cups.

SWEET TOPPING
Apple Butter

The best part of making apple butter is that your house fills with a sweet, cinnamon aroma. It isn't a lot of work, but it takes a long time to bake, so plan to make it when you are working around the house. Nothing tastes better spread on muffins, scones, or toast.

10	apples
1	cup apple cider
1/4	teaspoon nutmeg
1/4	teaspoon allspice
1/2	teaspoon cinnamon

Peel and core the apples, then cut them into 1-inch chunks. Place the chunks in a large, nonreactive saucepan with the cider. Cover the pot and cook over low heat until the apples are soft, about 30 minutes. Mix together the nutmeg, allspice, and cinnamon.

When the apples are soft, remove them from the heat, cool, and then divide them into two batches. Puree each batch in a food processor or blender. Pour all of the pureed fruit into a 13- by 9- by 2-inch baking dish, sprinkle with the spice mix, and stir well.

Stirring every 20 minutes, bake in a preheated 300° oven for 2 to 3 hours, or until your apple butter is deep brown and thick. Cool and then scoop it into a clean jar with a sealable lid. It will keep for up to 2 months in your refrigerator. Makes 1 1/2 cups.

Applesauce Muffins

These cinnamon-spiced muffins are made with chunky applesauce instead of sliced apples. Enjoy them on a crisp fall morning or pack them into lunch boxes.

INGREDIENTS

1 1/2	cups flour
1	teaspoon baking powder
1/2	teaspoon baking soda
1	teaspoon cinnamon
1/2	teaspoon salt
2	eggs
2/3	cup brown sugar
1 1/2	cups chunky applesauce
6	tablespoons butter, melted

1 Heat the oven to 375°. Grease a 12-cup muffin pan (or line it with paper bake cups) and set aside.

2 Sift together the flour, baking powder, baking soda, cinnamon, and salt into a large mixing bowl.

3 In another large bowl, beat together the eggs and brown sugar. Stir in the applesauce and melted butter until the mixture is smooth.

4 Pour the apple mixture over the flour mixture. Mix with a wooden spoon until combined (it's ready when you can't see any traces of flour).

5 Fill the bake cups about two thirds full with batter (an ice-cream scoop works well for this task). Bake until light brown, about 20 minutes. Test for doneness by inserting a knife in the middle of one muffin. If it comes out clean, the muffins are done. Makes 12.

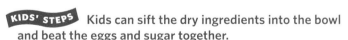 Kids can sift the dry ingredients into the bowl and beat the eggs and sugar together.

PREP TIME: **20 minutes**   BAKING TIME: **about 25 minutes**

Blueberry Buckle Muffins

Sprinkled with a sweet crumb topping, these muffins — bursting with blueberries — taste like mini coffee cakes.

TOPPING

- ⅓ cup sugar
- ½ cup flour
- 1½ teaspoons cinnamon
- ¼ cup butter, room temperature

BATTER

- ¼ cup butter, room temperature
- ¾ cup sugar
- 2 eggs
- ½ cup milk
- 1 teaspoon vanilla extract
- 2 cups flour
- 2 teaspoons baking powder
- ¼ teaspoon salt
- 2 cups blueberries, stemmed and rinsed

1 Heat the oven to 350° and line a 12-cup muffin pan with paper bake cups.

2 To make the topping, mix together the sugar, flour, and cinnamon. Work the butter in until the mixture is crumbly, then set aside.

3 In a large mixing bowl, cream the butter and the sugar. Beat in the eggs, then the milk and vanilla extract.

4 Sift the flour, baking powder, and salt into a medium mixing bowl. Pour over the wet ingredients and stir well, but don't overmix. Fold in the berries. Spoon the batter into the muffin cups (an ice-cream scoop also works well for this task), filling each cup about three quarters full. Generously sprinkle the crumb topping on each muffin.

5 Bake until the muffins are lightly brown and a knife inserted in the middle of one comes out clean, about 20 to 25 minutes. Makes 12.

KIDS' STEPS Kids can measure the ingredients, stir the batter, and sprinkle the topping on each muffin.

Churn Your Own Butter

• • • • • • • • • • • • • • • • • • • •

"My husband Peter, daughters Grace, 11, Charlotte, 6, and I have a Thanksgiving morning tradition of making butter together. We pull out a special plastic jar decorated with holiday stickers, drop in 3 clean marbles, and pour in a half-pint of heavy cream. Sitting in a tight circle, we each take turns shaking the jar vigorously as we talk about what we are thankful for. It usually takes about 10 minutes of dedicated shaking (and Peter and I do the bulk of the work) before we hear the telltale thunk that tells us we have butter.

"After removing the marbles and adding a touch of salt, we put the butter into a ramekin and place it on the Thanksgiving table. Our girls are so proud to serve the homemade butter at the table that evening."

— *Martha Browning*
Los Angeles, California

PREP TIME: 25 minutes   **BAKING TIME:** about 15 minutes

Raisin Scones

Kids can use a variety of cookie cutters to give these scones different shapes. Just make sure the scones are all about the same size so they cook evenly.

INGREDIENTS

- 2   cups flour
- 2   tablespoons sugar
- 2   teaspoons baking powder
- 1/2 teaspoon salt
- 3/4 teaspoon cinnamon (optional)
- 4   tablespoons butter
- 1   cup (about 5 ounces) raisins
- 2   eggs
- 1/2 cup milk

1 Combine the flour, sugar, baking powder, salt, and cinnamon in a large mixing bowl. Blend in the butter with a fork until the mixture is crumbly. Stir in the raisins. In a separate bowl, beat the eggs, then stir in the milk.

2 Make a well in the middle of the dry mixture and pour the egg mixture into it. Stir just until blended. Turn the dough onto a floured surface, knead a few times, then pat into a 3/4-inch thickness.

3 Cut out 14 to 15 scones using a cookie cutter or a butter knife. Bake on an ungreased cookie sheet at 400° for 12 to 15 minutes. Serve warm. Makes 14 to 15 medium scones.

KIDS' STEPS Kids can mix the dry ingredients, beat the eggs, and use the cookie cutters to make the scones different shapes.

Jammy Scones

Sweet and light, these scones can be gobbled up without any extra condiments, since the jam is baked right in. Use your favorite jam, or try the homemade version at right.

INGREDIENTS

- 3 cups flour
- 1/2 cup sugar
- 2 teaspoons baking powder
- 1/2 teaspoon baking soda
- 1 teaspoon salt
- 14 tablespoons (1 3/4 sticks) butter, cut into small pieces
- 1 cup buttermilk
- 1/4 cup of your favorite jam

1 Heat the oven to 425°. In a large bowl, combine the flour, sugar, baking powder, baking soda, and salt. Use a pastry cutter or two knives to cut in the butter until the dough resembles coarse cornmeal. Avoid overhandling the dough.

2 Add the buttermilk and combine with a fork, then use your hands to gather, as best you can, the crumbly dough into a ball.

3 Pat out the dough on a lightly floured surface and form it into an 8- by 10-inch rectangle 1 inch thick. Spread jam on half the rectangle lengthwise. Using a spatula if necessary, fold the other half onto the jammed half and roll out into a long rectangular shape about 1 inch thick. Cut the dough into 12 squares.

4 Place the scones 1 inch apart on an ungreased cookie sheet (wax paper-lined for easier cleanup) and bake until golden on top, about 15 minutes. Makes 12.

KIDS' STEPS Kids can gather the dough into a ball, spread on the jam, and cut it into squares.

SWEET TOPPING
Two-Berry Refrigerator Jam

Cooked jams don't get much easier than this one. Although the jam takes several hours to set, the preparation takes only a few minutes from berry to jar.

- 1 pint hulled and cleaned strawberries
- 1 cup cleaned red raspberries
- 1 cup sugar
- 3 tablespoons powdered fruit pectin
- 1 tablespoon lemon juice
- 2 8-ounce canning jars with lids (thoroughly washed and dried)

Cut the strawberries in half, then put all the berries in a large saucepan, preferably nonstick.

Gently crush the berries just 2 or 3 times with a potato masher. Stir in the sugar, pectin, and lemon juice. Stirring continually, gradually bring the mixture to a full boil and continue boiling it for 5 minutes. Remove the pan from the heat and divide the jam between the 2 containers, leaving at least 1/4 inch of air space at the top.

Screw on the lids and let the jars cool. Once they've reached room temperature, let them set for several hours more, then refrigerate them. Don't expect the fruit to firm up immediately; it will thicken as it chills. The jam will last for at least a couple of weeks in the refrigerator. Makes 2 cups.

PREP TIME: **about 30 minutes**   BAKING TIME: **about 40 minutes**

Streusel Coffee Cake

Moist, buttery, and packed inside and out with brown sugar streusel, this recipe is great for aspiring bakers, with lots of measuring, mixing, and other fun cooking jobs.

CINNAMON CRUNCH TOPPING

1 1/2	cups pecans or walnuts
1/3	cup packed light brown sugar
2	tablespoons flour
1	teaspoon cinnamon
3	tablespoons cold unsalted butter, cut into pieces

SOUR CREAM CAKE

2 3/4	cups flour
2	teaspoons baking powder
1/2	teaspoon baking soda
1/2	teaspoon salt
1	cup unsalted butter, softened
1 3/4	cups sugar
3	eggs, at room temperature
1	teaspoon grated lemon zest
1	teaspoon vanilla extract
3/4	cup sour cream
1/2	cup milk

SWEET GLAZE

1 1/4	cups confectioners' sugar
2	tablespoons milk

1 Heat the oven to 350°. Butter and flour a 9- by 13- by 2-inch cake pan.

2 To prepare the topping, coarsely chop the nuts, then combine them in a bowl with the brown sugar, flour, and cinnamon, and mix. Cut in the butter with a pastry cutter until the mixture resembles coarse crumbs.

3 To make the cake, sift the flour, baking powder, baking soda, and salt into a medium bowl and set it aside. Using an electric mixer (preferably a large stand mixer) cream the butter, then gradually add the sugar. Add the eggs one at a time, beating well after each addition. Add the lemon zest and vanilla and blend briefly.

4 Whisk together the sour cream and milk. Mix about a third of the mixture into the creamed ingredients until smooth. Then blend in about a third of the flour mixture. Continue alternately beating in the liquid and dry ingredients by thirds.

5 Spread half the batter in the prepared pan. Evenly sprinkle half the topping on it, pressing it lightly into the batter. Spread the remaining batter evenly over the topping. Then cover that layer with the remaining topping. Bake on the center oven rack until nicely browned, about 40 minutes. A toothpick inserted at the center should come out clean. Place the pan on a wire rack and let the cake cool completely.

6 For the glaze, combine the confectioners' sugar and milk in a large bowl and whisk until smooth and suitable to drizzle. If needed, you can make the glaze thinner or thicker by adding a little more milk or sugar, respectively. Use a spoon to drizzle the glaze on the cooled coffee cake. Serves 12 or more.

KIDS' STEPS Kids can toss the nut topping mixture together, measure and mix the dry ingredients, and make the glaze.

Homemade Granola

INGREDIENTS

- 4 cups rolled oats
- 1 cup wheat germ
- 1 cup chopped walnuts or slivered almonds
- 1/2 cup sesame seeds
- 1/4 cup brown sugar
- 1 teaspoon cinnamon
- 1/4 teaspoon salt
- 1/3 cup vegetable oil
- 1/3 cup honey
- 1/3 cup water
- 1 package (6-ounce) dried sweetened cranberries or other dried fruit such as cherries, raisins, pineapple, or papaya

Crunchy, nutty, and just sweet enough, this granola is the best we've ever tasted. The recipe makes plenty, so store some for the whole week.

1 Heat the oven to 300°. In a large mixing bowl, stir together the oats, wheat germ, nuts, sesame seeds, brown sugar, cinnamon, and salt.

2 Make a well in the dry ingredients and add the oil, honey, and water.

3 Toss the mixture until the ingredients are well combined, then spread it evenly in a large baking pan.

4 Bake the granola for 40 minutes or until lightly browned, stirring every 10 minutes to keep the mixture from sticking. Let it cool completely, then stir in the cranberries or dried fruit. Makes about 7 cups.

KIDS' STEPS Kids can measure the ingredients into a bowl and spread the mixture into the baking pan.

Quick Oats

Let kids mix up individual servings of healthy instant hot cereal, then keep a stash on hand for those hurried school mornings.

INGREDIENTS

- 4 cups rolled oats (not quick-cooking)
- 3/4 teaspoon salt
- 6 resealable plastic bags

  Flavoring of your choice (see below)

  Milk (optional)

1 Combine the rolled oats and salt in a food processor or blender and grind them (in 2 batches, if necessary) to the consistency of wheat germ.

2 Scoop ½-cup portions into each bag. Flavor each one (try our mix-ins below, or make up your own combinations), then seal the bags and shake them to mix.

3 When it's time to eat, empty the contents of 1 bag into a bowl and slowly stir in 1 cup of boiling water. Cover and let it sit for 3 minutes. Stir again and add a splash of milk, if you like. Makes 6 servings.

CINNAMON RAISIN
1 teaspoon of sugar, 1 tablespoon of raisins, and a dash of cinnamon

BROWN SUGAR SPICE
1 teaspoon of packed brown sugar and a dash each of ground cinnamon, nutmeg, and clove

PECAN PIE
1 teaspoon of packed brown sugar and 1 tablespoon of chopped pecans

APPLE CHERRY
1 teaspoon of packed brown sugar and 1 tablespoon each of chopped dried cherries and apples

 KIDS' STEPS Kids can mix the oats and fill the bags.

CHAPTER TWO

LUNCH

Shake up the lunch routine with ideas that make the grade

WHEN IT COMES TO MIDDAY MEALS, it's easy to get in a rut. Peanut butter and jelly. Grilled cheese. Bologna on white bread. Familiar favorites may simplify lunch prep, but nothing wears out a sandwich's appeal like serving it day after day. In this chapter, you'll find quick, nutritious alternatives for school or home. In a rush? Whip up our Cracker Sandwiches or Assemble-at-School Sub, or cut out some Cookie-Cutter Cheese Toasts and let them do double duty as a hot lunch today and a cold lunch-box meal tomorrow. Here are some other lunch tips from the readers of *FamilyFun*.

PICK THEIR FAVORITES. To solve the school-lunch crunch, *FamilyFun* reader Christina Calderaio of Warrington, Pennsylvania, has her children mark their choices on a homemade menu. Dee Martin of Cleveland, Ohio, makes the sandwiches, then lets her kids choose one item from each of three baskets containing fruits, vegetables, and snacks. The bottom line? Giving kids a say in the process is the best way to ensure they'll actually eat what you pack.

ADD A NEW DIMENSION. Jeanine Manser of Elgin, Illinois, keeps her daughter's lunches lively with an occasional themed meal. Over the years, she has created teeny tiny tea parties (finger sandwiches, grapes,

and mini muffins on doll plates), round meals (a bagel and cream cheese, an orange, and circular carrot slices), and winter-themed spreads (a snowman-shaped sandwich, carrot noses, and hot chocolate), as well as lunches themed around colors, holidays, shapes, and even countries.

PACK A SURPRISE. Many *FamilyFun* readers send a little bit of home in their kids' lunch boxes, such as a note or sticker. Karen Jameson of Valencia, California, adds a sheet from a page-a-day joke calendar. And Ella Graney of Fort Wayne, Indiana, created a simple lunch box memo board by sticking a piece of Con-Tact paper under the lid, where she writes silly notes and riddles.

Peanut Butter and Jelly Pizza

For a quick lunch or after-school snack, invite your kids to assemble this no-cook "pizza." Like its cheesy cousin, this one can be customized with favorite toppings.

INGREDIENTS

3   tablespoons peanut butter (creamy or crunchy)

1   whole pita bread (medium-size)

    Toppings, such as jelly, raisins, grated apples, sliced bananas, Cheerios, and peanuts

1 Spread the peanut butter "sauce" on the pita bread. Then top the pizza with jelly, raisins, Cheerios, grated apples, and/or banana slices. You can arrange the toppings randomly or in a pattern.

2 Help your older child use a pizza cutter to slice the pizza into wedges. Grip the pizza cutter handle firmly, apply slight pressure, and roll the blade steadily and in a straight line. Serves 1 to 2.

KIDS' STEPS Kids can spread the peanut butter on the pita. Older kids can use a pizza cutter to slice the "pie."

IS YOUR CHILD'S CLASSROOM A PEANUT-FREE ZONE?
Even a whiff of a peanut product can trigger a reaction in children with severe peanut allergies, so many schools now ban the legumes completely. Check your school's policy before sending any peanutty treats to class.

Star Sandwiches

There's no doubt that PB & J has star status among kids. Our version encourages kids to dress up the classic sandwich by punching star shapes out of the bread.

INGREDIENTS

- 2   slices white bread
- 2   slices whole wheat bread
-     1½-inch star cookie cutter
-     Peanut butter and jelly

1 For each sandwich, use a star cookie cutter to cut two stars out of a slice of the white bread and two stars out of a slice of the whole wheat bread. Then fit the whole wheat stars into the star-shaped holes in the white bread and the white stars into the whole wheat bread.

2 Now the bread is ready for the peanut butter and jelly. Have your child use a table knife to smoothly spread on peanut butter and jelly, working slowly to avoid tearing the bread. Assemble the sandwiches, then wrap in plastic. Makes 2 star-studded sandwiches.

KIDS' STEPS   Kids can cut the stars out with the cookie cutter and spread on the peanut butter and jelly.

TIP: Firmly press the cookie cutter into the bread, then gently remove and swap the stars.

COOKING BASICS
My Own Peanut Butter

Teach your child to use a food processor while mixing up this peanut butter recipe. It makes enough for about a dozen sandwiches.

- 2   cups unsalted dry-roasted peanuts
- 3   to 4 tablespoons vegetable oil
- ¼   teaspoon salt

Pour the peanuts into the bowl of a food processor. Process until they are finely chopped.

Add the vegetable oil one tablespoon at a time, processing until the peanut butter begins to form a ball. Add the salt and process until well combined. Transfer to a clean jar with a lid.

Decorate a large white mailing label before affixing it to the jar. Store in the refrigerator for up to 2 weeks. If the oil separates from the nut butter, stir before using. Makes 1 cup.

Pocket Full of Rulers

When it comes to presentation — which often is the key to getting kids to eat — this stuffed pocket really measures up. The veggies that fill it are cut to resemble mini ruler shapes.

MY GREAT IDEA

Make a Chart

• •

Liz Ruff of West Chester, Pennsylvania, didn't want to get into a classic morning debate over who would take what for lunch. So she asked sons Bobby, 11, Joey, 9, Matt, 7, and Timmy, 4, to post a list of favorite foods on the fridge. The boys agreed to eat what their mom packs, as long as it's on the list.

The chart turned up some surprises, says mom Liz. "I had an idea Joey liked granola, but was surprised when he said he always trades for it with his friend at school." The boys also make note of their changing tastes, which is part of the system's strength: "The boys know what they like to eat matters."

INGREDIENTS

Assorted fresh vegetables (cucumbers, carrots, avocados, peppers, and so on)

Pita bread

Lettuce

Croutons (optional)

Salad dressing

1 Scrub and peel the vegetables. Lay each one on a cutting board and slice it lengthwise into thin, rulerlike shapes.

2 Cut off the top of the pita bread and line the inside with lettuce. Fill the pocket with the ruler veggies and tightly cover the sandwich with plastic wrap.

3 Pack the pita with a small baggie filled with croutons, if desired, and a small container of salad dressing.

KIDS' STEPS Kids can scrub the vegetables and arrange them in the pita.

PREP TIME: 10 minutes

Cracker Sandwiches

Even kids who prefer nibbling to eating a big meal need a lunch that will stick to their ribs. This light sandwich alternative consists of tasty tidbits and crackers to stick together with cream cheese glue.

INGREDIENTS

Whipped cream cheese

Assorted fresh vegetables, such as green beans, edible pea pods, carrot slices, and chopped celery (avoid vegetables like cucumbers that tend to get juicy when sliced)

Sliced or cubed ham or turkey

Crackers

KIDS' STEPS Kids can assemble the cracker sandwiches.

1 Pack the cream cheese in a small sealable plastic container (don't forget to include a plastic knife or craft stick for spreading).

2 Arrange the veggies and meat in another container and pack the crackers separately as well.

3 At lunchtime, your child needs only to pop open the containers and assemble her cracker creations. Serves 1.

MY GREAT IDEA
Make a Deal

• • • • • • • • • • • • • • • • • • • •

When Cathy Hunter of Zionsville, Indiana, was in sixth grade, her mother, Marilyn, upped her allowance to $10 a week and struck a deal with her: buy lunch at school and pay for it yourself, or pack it at home and pocket the money. "I don't think she ever bought a lunch," says Marilyn. "She really got into the extra money." More importantly, the system stopped any disagreement over what to eat for lunch. A great bonus was Cathy's interest in meal planning and preparation. "She was always in the recipe books looking for things she could make," says Marilyn, "and by the time she was in high school she was making our dinners."

Sandwich Sensations

• • • • • • • • • • • • • • • • • • • •

Englishman John Montagu, Fourth Earl of Sandwich, is credited with inventing the sandwich when he needed a quick and easy meal. Still popular more than 200 years later, the sandwich lends itself to many tasty variations, including the following:

CALIFORNIA VEGGIE
Spread herb cream cheese on multigrain bread, then add lettuce, tomato, grated carrot, alfalfa sprouts, and slices of avocado and cucumber.

FAJITA WRAP Roll up strips of grilled chicken breast, salsa, refried beans, lettuce, and shredded pepper Jack cheese in a warm tortilla.

REUBEN Pile hot corned beef or pastrami (called a Rachel), Swiss cheese, and sauerkraut atop grilled rye bread and smother with Thousand Island dressing.

PREP TIME: 10 minutes

Assemble-at-School Sub

To prevent soggy sandwiches, pack up the fixings for a sub and let your chef make a fresh one at school.

INGREDIENTS

Sandwich fillings, such as lettuce, black olives, onions, cherry tomatoes

Cheese, such as Provolone or Muenster

Deli meat, such as salami, turkey, or ham

Oblong sub roll or baguette section

Italian dressing, mustard, or mayonnaise

1 Shred the lettuce, chop the olives, and slice the onions with a chef's knife (parents and older kids only). Wash and dry the cherry tomatoes. Line up the vegetables in rows in a sealable plastic container. Roll up the cheese and the meat and place in the container next to the veggies.

2 Pour the dressing into a small plastic container or gather packets of mustard or mayonnaise.

3 Pack the fillings, the dressing, a sub roll wrapped in plastic, and a plastic knife (for slicing the tomatoes and spreading the mustard or mayo) in a lunch box.

4 At school, your child can build a sub sandwich or just eat the fillings as an antipasto.

KIDS' STEPS Kids can line up the vegetables in the plastic container, roll the lunch meat, and assemble their sandwich at school.

Silly Sandwiches

Help your kids put together a lunch that has a lot of personality.

INGREDIENTS

Sandwich roll

Condiments, such as mustard, mayonnaise, or Italian dressing

Cold cuts, such as roast beef, ham, turkey, and cheese

Raw vegetables, such as cucumbers, carrots, tomatoes, olives, and green peppers

Softened cream cheese

1 Spread your favorite condiment on the bottom half of a sandwich roll.

2 Add a slice of ham or another cold cut. Then fold a second slice of meat lengthwise so that it resembles a tongue and lay it across the bun with one end hanging over the edge, as shown.

3 Create a face on the bun top using sliced raw vegetables. Use the softened cream cheese for glue. (The veggies stick best if you first blot them dry with a paper towel.) You can even add a couple of cheese cube "teeth."

4 Push bell pepper slices into the bun for a spiky hairdo, or adorn it with carrot curls made using a potato peeler.

KIDS' STEPS Kids can assemble the sandwich and use the vegetables to make funny faces.

MY GREAT IDEA
Send a Momable

• •

When Jenni Uhe came home from school begging for the prepackaged mini lunch sets of meats, cheese, and crackers, her mom Monica priced them out. "She cried because we couldn't get them," she recalls.

Then Monica came up with an idea. She got out her cookie cutters and some sectional plastic containers, and invited Jenni to help her make a homemade Lunchable. Monica went so far as to write "Momable" on the plastic lid with permanent marker. The result made such a splash at school that Jenni was instantly won over — Monica was fielding calls from other parents, wondering where they, too, could buy Momables.

PREP TIME: **10 minutes**

Spiral Sandwiches

Kids get a kick out of these elegant roll-ups that show off a food design inside. Give the young chefs lots of elbow room and tell them to take their time rolling it up.

INGREDIENTS

- ½ cup cream cheese, at room temperature
- 4 chives, 1 sprig of dill, and/or 3 basil leaves (optional)
- 6 spinach leaves
- 2 large flour tortillas
- 1 tomato, seeded and sliced into thin rounds

1 Place the cream cheese in a small bowl. For herb cream cheese, use scissors to snip the herbs into tiny pieces, then mash them into the cream cheese.

2 Spread a little cream cheese on each of the spinach leaves, then spread the remainder in a thin layer onto one side of each tortilla. Place three tomato slices in a row down the middle. Top with the spinach leaves, cream cheese facing up.

3 Roll up each tortilla tightly into a log. Pinch the seams shut. Use a serrated knife to slowly slice each log crosswise into 5 or 6 pinwheel sandwiches. Serves 2 to 4.

KIDS' STEPS Kids can mix the herbs into the cream cheese, layer the tortilla with the fixings, and roll up the sandwich.

MY GREAT IDEA
Vary the Bread

Susan Freeman of Ames, Iowa, beats the lunchtime blahs by eliminating the obvious. Instead of regular bread, she makes turkey and PB & J sandwiches on pita, bagels, English muffins, hot dog rolls, or even hamburger buns. Or, she rolls them up in a tortilla and serves them whole or sliced into pinwheels.

PREP TIME: **10 minutes**

Snail Snack

This silly-looking snack may appear to be moving at a snail's pace, but it goes together — and disappears — quick as a wink.

INGREDIENTS

- Mayonnaise or whipped cream cheese
- Large tortilla (square, if available)
- Lettuce or baby spinach
- Sliced deli meat of your choice
- Sliced cheese of your choice
- Gherkin pickles
- Chive stalks

1 If necessary, trim the rounded edges of the tortilla to make it square, then spread on a thin layer of the mayonnaise or cream cheese.

2 Layer on the lettuce or spinach, then the meat and cheese and roll it up tightly.

3 With the seam on the bottom, slice the tortilla into 2-inch-wide pinwheels. For the snails' heads, cut a pickle in half at an angle. Poke 2 small holes in the uncut ends and stick pieces of chive with knots at one end in each for antennae.

4 Slip each pickle half under the edge of a pinwheel, securing them together with a toothpick, if necessary. Makes 4 to 6 pinwheel sandwiches.

KIDS' STEPS Kids can layer and roll up the sandwich and position the pickle "head" under the pinwheel sandwich.

Poached Chicken

Poaching meat means to simmer it in liquid. This method creates moist chicken, perfect for making chicken salad.

Place a small quartered onion (optional) and 1½ pounds of boneless, skinless chicken breast (enough to yield the 3 cups needed for each recipe at right) in a saucepan, cover with water, and cook over high heat. Once the water boils, reduce the heat and simmer for 20 minutes. Check the chicken for doneness (the center should be white with no traces of pink).

Transfer the chicken from the water to a cutting board and let it cool before chopping it into chunks. Let the chicken cool completely before making your salad.

PREP TIME: 15 minutes   **COOKING TIME:** 25 minutes

Curried Chicken Salad

Here's a variation on chicken salad that has a bit of a kick, and a couple of other surprises, too: grapes for a sweet accent and cashews for crunch.

INGREDIENTS

- ½ cup mayonnaise
- ½ cup sour cream
- 1 tablespoon lemon juice
- 2 to 3 teaspoons curry powder
- ½ teaspoon Dijon mustard
- 3 cups cooked, cubed chicken breast (see recipe at left)
- ¾ cup halved or quartered green grapes
- ½ cup chopped roasted cashews

  Salt and ground black pepper to taste
- 2 or 3 pita breads

  Leaf lettuce

1 In a small bowl, blend the mayonnaise, sour cream, lemon juice, curry powder, and mustard and then set aside.

2 Combine the chicken, grapes, and cashews in a large bowl. Add the dressing and mix well. Salt and pepper the chicken salad to taste.

3 To assemble the sandwiches, halve the pita breads and place a couple of lettuce leaves inside each half. Spoon in the chicken salad and serve. Makes 4 to 6 sandwiches.

KIDS' STEPS Kids can remove grapes from stalks, blend the mayonnaise mix together, and stuff the pitas.

PREP TIME: 10 minutes   **COOKING TIME:** 25 minutes

Tea Sandwiches

These mild-flavored chicken salad sandwiches are perfect for a children's tea party. They look divine served on a fancy paper doily.

INGREDIENTS

- 3 cups cooked, cubed chicken breast (see recipe at left)
- ½ to ¾ cup mayonnaise
- 20 green grapes

  Salt and pepper, to taste
- ½ teaspoon tarragon
- ⅓ cup slivered almonds (optional)

  Thin sandwich bread

1 Combine the chicken chunks with the mayonnaise and toss well. Slice the grapes and add them to the bowl, then stir in salt, pepper, and tarragon. Stir in the almonds, if desired.

2 Remove the crusts from two slices of bread, add the chicken salad filling, and cut into triangles. Makes 8 full-size sandwiches (32 tea sandwiches).

KIDS' STEPS Kids can remove grapes from stalks, mix the chicken salad together, and cut the crusts off the bread.

Top Turkey Sandwiches

Here we've gathered some of our favorite turkey sandwich combinations. Some are perfect for using up leftovers, while others can be made straight from the deli.

THANKSGIVING SPECIAL
Layer your leftover fixings — sliced turkey, cranberry sauce, and stuffing — on some sturdy white bread.

THE CAESAR WRAP
Have a salad and a sandwich all in one with this refreshing wrap. Just line a large flour tortilla with sliced turkey, shredded romaine, diced tomatoes, shredded Parmesan cheese, and creamy Caesar dressing.

TURKEY PARMIGIANA
Great with thick slices from leftover turkey, this hot sandwich hits the spot. Layer turkey, spaghetti sauce, and shredded mozzarella atop crusty Italian bread and place under the broiler until hot.

TURKEY HI-RISE
A traditional club sandwich has 3 slices of toast, but we find 2 is plenty piled high with sliced turkey, bacon, lettuce, tomato, and mayonnaise.

TURKEY REUBEN
A white meat version of the famous corned beef sandwich, this grilled lunch is just as good. Pile turkey, sauerkraut, and Swiss cheese on rye bread and grill. Serve with Thousand Island dressing.

THE CALIFORNIA ROLL-UP
As tasty as it is colorful, this West Coast–inspired wrap has turkey, lettuce, tomato, avocado, alfalfa sprouts, and shredded Jack cheese rolled in a large flour tortilla.

KIDS' STEPS Kids can help with all the sandwiches, washing lettuce, slicing an avocado, and layering the wraps.

PREP TIME: **15 minutes**   COOKING TIME: **10 minutes**

Southwestern Club Wrap

These club sandwich-like roll-ups are great for a summer lunch with friends or to bring to a potluck.

INGREDIENTS

4   to 6 large flour tortillas
¾   cup ranch dressing
⅓   cup barbecue sauce
¼   head iceberg lettuce, very thinly sliced
     Handful of cherry tomatoes, quartered
½   pound pepper Jack or Monterey Jack cheese, grated
1   ripe avocado, thinly sliced
1   cup pitted black olives, chopped
1   cup red bell peppers, chopped
½   pound smoked or buffalo-style turkey, thinly sliced

1 Heat the oven to 250°. Wrap the tortillas in aluminum foil and warm them in the oven for about 10 minutes to soften. This will make them easier to roll. Alternately, heat each tortilla in the microwave for 10 seconds.

2 Make the sauce by combining the ranch dressing and barbecue sauce in a small bowl and stir until blended.

3 Working with one wrapper at a time, layer each ingredient on half of the tortilla. Start with a bit of sauce (there'll be plenty left to serve on the side as well), then add the lettuce, tomatoes, cheese, avocado, olives, and peppers, using as much of each as you like, but not so much that the sandwich will be difficult to roll. End with a piece of the turkey. Fold in each side of the tortilla and begin rolling the wrap from the end with the filling. Tuck in the filling as you roll.

4 Slice each sandwich in the center, on the bias, with a sharp serrated knife and serve (with the extra sauce in a bowl). Makes 4 to 6 wraps.

KIDS' STEPS Kids can mix up the sauce and line the wraps with their favorite fillings.

MY GREAT IDEA
Get in the Spirit
• •

Sometimes the best ideas sneak up on you. For *FamilyFun* reader Rivana Stadtlander of Aventura, Florida, one came a few years ago while packing school lunch for her daughter, Alivia, then age three.

As Rivana cast about for a napkin to toss in with Alivia's lunch, she spied a stack of leftover party napkins and started using them. One morning, when the napkins finally ran out, she resorted to plain napkins. Uh-oh. Alivia came home disappointed, asking, "Where was the special napkin of the day?" To Rivana, they were just napkins. To Alivia, they were neat treats — and her friends missed them too!

A tradition was born. Since then, Rivana watches for playful napkins on sale and stocks up on themes dear to her daughter's heart.

Bagel Critters

At lunchtime, let your kids turn bagels, cream cheese, and assorted toppings into an edible zoo. This playful recipe also works well as an activity and quick lunch at a birthday party.

INGREDIENTS

Bagels, sliced

Cream cheese, softened

Assorted toppings, such as baby carrots (grated or whole), cherry tomato halves, sliced black olives, sliced bell pepper (red, green, or yellow), poppy seeds, cucumber rounds, minced chives, and crunchy Chinese noodles

1 Spread the cream cheese on the cut bagels (going gently over the hole).

2 Set out bowls of vegetables and crunchy noodles and let the kids turn the bagels into animal or monster faces like the royal lion (left) with olive eyes and nose, a crunchy noodle mane and whiskers, poppy seed freckles, and a pepper crown.

KIDS' STEPS Kids can spread on the cream cheese and decorate the bagel.

QUICK TRICK
Family Portrait Bagels

Celebrate your family by making a delicious, edible family portrait on bagels. Moms and dads can make their self-portraits on regular-size bagels; kids can create theirs on mini bagels.

Begin with a bagel covered with cream cheese. Next, create the family member's likeness with anything from blueberries to tomatoes and chives. Set them together on a plate — and don't forget to take a family photo! Here's what we used on the bagels at left:

MOM Lox hair, black-olive eyes, parsley lashes, red-pepper lips, and a carrot nose.

GIRL Carrot hair, chive hair ribbon, green-pepper eyes, chopped-peanut freckles, and grape-tomato mouth.

BOY Chive hair, carrot-and-black-olive eyes, and tomato mouth.

Butterfly Cheese-wich

Turn an ordinary grilled cheese into something special with this butterfly sandwich.

QUICK TRICK
Cookie-Cutter Cheese Toasts

Kids like these treats because they look like cookies; parents like them because they aren't. Serve them warm or cold; they're terrific either way.

Heat the oven or toaster oven to 350°. Place 2 slices of whole wheat bread on a cookie sheet or toaster-oven tray and top each with a slice of cheese. Cut out shapes using cookie cutters.

Place the "cookies" in the oven and heat until the cheese melts. Serve warm or place in plastic bags when cool for a portable snack.

INGREDIENTS
- 1 pat butter
- 2 slices bread
- 2 slices cheese

  Vegetables, such as celery, cherry tomatoes, carrots, and peppers

1 Melt the pat of butter in a frying pan.

2 Assemble and grill the sandwich as you would a regular grilled cheese, then cut out the wings as shown. Place a celery stick in the center for the butterfly's body, poke cherry tomatoes onto carrot sticks for antennae, then add carrot or pepper spots. Makes 1 butterfly.

KIDS' STEPS Kids can cut the sandwich into wings with a plastic knife and create a butterfly body with vegetables.

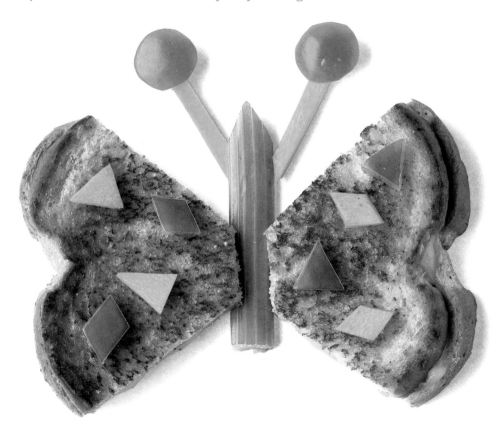

Pesto, Cheese, and Chicken Meltdown

Pesto is so delicious kids are willing to try it on just about anything, like this grilled cheese and chicken sandwich.

> 2 slices fresh Italian bread (about 3/4 inch thick)
>
> 2 tablespoons pesto sauce, store-bought or homemade
>
> 2 slices Provolone or sharp Cheddar cheese
>
> 2 or 3 thin slices deli chicken or turkey
>
> 2 or 3 thin slices ripe tomato (optional)
>
> 1 tablespoon softened butter

Spread 1 tablespoon of the pesto on each of the bread slices. Then build the sandwich on one of the slices, first layering on 1 slice of cheese and then the chicken or turkey. Add the tomato if you're using it, followed by the last slice of cheese. Press the other piece of bread, pesto side down, onto the sandwich.

Place a frying pan or skillet over moderate heat. Meanwhile, spread half of the softened butter on both outer surfaces of the sandwich. Carefully place the sandwich in the heated pan and grill it on each side for about 3 to 3 1/2 minutes, until golden brown. Makes 1 sandwich.

PREP TIME: 10 minutes

Sweet Grilled Cheese

You won't have to say "cheese" to make your kids smile once they sample this lunch look-alike, which makes for a great April Fool's gag.

INGREDIENTS

> Pound cake (we used Entenmann's brand)
>
> 1 cup buttercream or white frosting
>
> Yellow and red food coloring

1 Cut the pound cake into breadlike slices and toast them in a toaster oven just until they turn golden brown. Once they've cooled, stack them by twos and cut each stack in half diagonally (slicing the cake before putting on the frosting filling makes for fewer crumbs).

2 Tint the frosting by stirring in a few drops of yellow and red food coloring (more yellow than red) to get a shade of orange that resembles American cheese.

3 Spread the frosting between the slices of each half sandwich. If you mound the frosting on one slice, then top it with the other and gently press down, the frosting will ooze out a bit and look all the more like melted cheese. Makes 1 sandwich.

KIDS' STEPS Kids can cut the cake and mix the frosting, then bring a few samples to school to fool their friends at lunchtime.

PREP TIME: 25 minutes BAKING TIME: 10 minutes

Easy Empanadas

These traditional Mexican treats can be eaten hot or cold. Try experimenting with different fillings, such as ground beef and grilled onions or ham and cheese.

INGREDIENTS

1½   cups flour
1   cup cornmeal
1   teaspoon baking powder
¼   teaspoon salt
1   teaspoon sugar
⅓   cup butter, softened
½   cup milk
1   cup salsa, strained
½   cup shredded cheese (pepper Jack adds a kick)

1 Heat the oven to 400°. Place the flour, cornmeal, baking powder, salt, sugar, and butter in a food processor fitted with a metal blade. Pulse until the ingredients are combined, about 2 minutes.

2 Slowly add the milk through the feed tube; mix until the dough forms a ball. If the dough is sticky, add more cornmeal.

3 Place half of the dough on a generously floured work surface and lightly flour the top of the dough as well. With a rolling pin, roll it out until it's an inch thick. With a cookie cutter (or a butter knife), cut the dough into 3- or 4-inch-diameter circles.

4 Stir together the salsa and cheese. Place approximately 1 teaspoon of the mixture in the center of every circle. Fold each circle in half and seal it by pressing around the edges with your fingers, then with the tines of a fork.

5 Place the empanadas on an ungreased baking sheet and bake them until golden brown, about 12 minutes. Repeat the process until all the dough has been used. Makes about 30.

KIDS' STEPS Kids can help roll out the dough, fill the empanadas, and seal them shut with their fingers.

· ·

PREP TIME: 10 minutes COOKING TIME: 10 minutes

Veggie Quesadilla

Oozing with warm melted cheese, quesadillas are great stuffed with nutritious vegetables.

INGREDIENTS

¼   cup grated carrot
¼   cup cooked and chopped broccoli
1   tablespoon chopped yellow or Vidalia onion (optional)
⅓   cup Monterey Jack or Cheddar cheese, shredded
½   teaspoon canola oil
1   large flour tortilla
1   tablespoon salsa or taco sauce

1 In a medium bowl, mix together the carrot, broccoli, onion (if desired), and cheese.

2 Set a large nonstick frying pan over medium heat and thinly coat the bottom of the pan with canola oil.

3 Place a tortilla in the pan, cover it with the cheese-veggie mixture, and drizzle the salsa or taco sauce on top. When the bottom of the tortilla is lightly browned and the cheese has melted, fold the quesadilla in half and transfer to a plate. Cut it into quarters and serve hot. Makes 1.

KIDS' STEPS Kids can grate the carrot and mix the vegetables and cheese together.

Basic Quiche

Rich and creamy, quiche has been a popular dish for hundreds of years and is still a big hit with kids.

PIE SHELL

- 1½ cups flour
- 1½ teaspoons sugar
- ½ teaspoon salt
- 6 tablespoons cold unsalted butter, cut into ¼-inch pieces
- 2 tablespoons vegetable shortening
- ⅓ cup ice-cold water

BASIC FILLING

- 3 eggs
- 1⅓ cups half-and-half or whole milk
- ½ teaspoon salt
- ¼ teaspoon black pepper
- 1 cup filling (see variations at right)
- 2 cups cheese (see variations at right)

1 Mix the flour, sugar, and salt in a large bowl. Add the butter and shortening, and toss again. Using a pastry blender, cut the fat into the flour until it is roughly the size of split peas.

2 Sprinkle the water over the mixture. Using a wooden spoon, briskly stir the pastry dough until it forms a shaggy ball. Transfer the ball to a lightly floured surface and knead it once or twice.

3 Place the pastry on a large piece of plastic wrap and flatten it into a ¾-inch-thick disk. Wrap the disk in the plastic and refrigerate it until firm, about 1 hour.

4 Lightly butter a 9½-inch deep-dish pie pan. Dust a large piece of waxed paper with flour and center the chilled pastry on it. With a floured rolling pin, roll the pastry into a 13-inch circle.

5 Invert the pastry over the pie pan and peel away the paper. Tuck the pastry into the pan without stretching it. Fold back the overhang, pinching it into a ridge, then freeze for 15 minutes. Heat the oven to 400°.

6 Line the chilled shell with aluminum foil (long enough so there is overhang on two sides). Press the foil into the bottom of the pan, then fill it halfway with dried beans or rice (to hold its shape). Bake for 20 minutes. Remove from the oven and grasp the foil to remove the beans.

7 Prick the bottom of the pastry 6 or 7 times with a fork, then put it back in the oven. Reduce the heat to 375° and bake the shell for 10 minutes more. Remove it from the oven and immediately sprinkle a handful of the cheese you are using over the fork holes, letting it melt to seal them. Set the shell on a cooling rack while you prepare the filling (see right).

8 Whisk the eggs, half-and-half, salt, and pepper in a large bowl. Spread your filling (but not the cheese) in the pie shell. Sprinkle on about half of the cheese. Ladle the egg mixture over the filling, then sprinkle on the remaining cheese.

9 Bake at 375° on the center oven rack until slightly puffy and golden brown, about 40 to 45 minutes. Transfer the pan to a wire rack and cool for at least 30 minutes. Serve warm, at room temperature, or cold. Be sure to refrigerate any leftovers. Makes 8 servings.

KIDS' STEPS Kids can sauté the vegetables. Younger ones can sprinkle on the cheese.

Quiche Fillings

BACON, SPINACH, AND CHEDDAR
Sautéed onion, garlic, and chopped spinach, 4 strips of crumbled crispy bacon, and Cheddar cheese.

BROCCOLI AND CHEESE
Broccoli florets (you can add them raw — they will cook while in the oven) and Cheddar cheese.

QUICHE LORRAINE
Thickly sliced cooked bacon (about 4 strips) and plain or Lorraine Swiss cheese.

CHAPTER THREE

SNACKS

From sweet to savory, serve up mini meals for kids on the go

SNACKS AREN'T JUST FAST FUEL for busy bodies. They're additional meals, providing a hefty chunk of the day's nutrition. But don't tell that to your kids! You'll find the easy, inexpensive recipes in this chapter walk the line perfectly — they pack a parent-approved healthy punch with a playful flair kids will love. Let your children help with the preparation and they'll think this food is even more fun. And whether you're staving off an after-school snack attack or whipping up a portable treat for the classroom, we suggest these tried-and-true tips.

LET YOUR SILLY SIDE SHINE. Fruits arranged like flowers, deviled egg sailboats, tomatoes with vegetable faces — the familiar becomes fresh when you give it a twist. Use our fanciful designs as a launching point for your own artistic inventions and watch those healthy treats disappear.

SET UP A SNACK STATION. Kids are never just hungry — they're starving. A drawer, basket, or refrigerator shelf stocked with quick treats like cheese cubes and cut veggies will keep them from hitting the cookie jar every time the munchies strike.

VEG OUT WITH VEGGIES. Try the Couch Potato Rule: the only snacks allowed in front of the TV are veggies in any form — except potato chips.

CREATE A "SNACKTIVITY." Offer your child apple slices and you may get a ho-hum reaction. But add a dab of peanut butter for dipping and suddenly you're serving not just a snack, but an activity. Use spreads, sauces, dips, and sprinkled toppings to make eating fun.

PACKAGE IT LIKE THE PROS. It's not just the sugar and salt that make store-bought snacks so appealing — it's the bells-and-whistles packaging. Stay competitive and present your munchables in clever containers, colorful plastic wrap, or jazz up your regular containers with stickers or permanent-marker designs. At home, try fancy dishware, unexpected utensils, and crazy straws.

Little Fruit-and-Cheese Kebabs

Here's further evidence that everything has more kid appeal when it is stuck on a stick. These delightfully simple kebabs can help satisfy a craving for sweets while providing good nutrition (protein, vitamins, and fiber).

INGREDIENTS

Fruit chunks (apples, pineapples, strawberries, and pears work well)
Cheddar cheese
Raisins
Toothpicks

1 Cut the fruit or fruits into cubes and slice the cheese into thick squares. Set the fruit and cheese out with the raisins and toothpicks.

2 Let your kids make tiny fruit, cheese, and raisin arrangements on the toothpicks in any order they like.

3 Eat the kebabs soon after you make them, when they're still nice and fresh.

KIDS' STEPS Kids can spear the fruit, cheese, and raisins with toothpicks.

PREP TIME: **15 minutes**   COOKING TIME: **15 minutes**

Easy Applesauce

Give your cache of fall apples a major supporting role by turning them into this delicious cinnamon-spiced applesauce.

INGREDIENTS

- 4 or 5 large apples, peeled, cored, and coarsely chopped
- 1 cup apple cider
- Pinch of salt
- ¼ to ⅓ cup sugar, to taste
- 1½ tablespoons lemon juice
- ¼ to ½ teaspoon cinnamon, to taste

1 Put the apples, cider, salt, and sugar in a large, nonreactive saucepan. Bring to a boil, then cover and reduce the heat to a low boil. Simmer the apples until tender, about 15 minutes. Be sure to check after 10 minutes to make sure there's enough liquid in the pan to keep the apples from sticking. When the apples are tender, remove the pan from the heat and let it cool for 15 minutes.

2 Transfer the apples and their juice to a food processor. Blend with the lemon juice and cinnamon to your desired consistency.

3 Pour the applesauce into a bowl and let it cool thoroughly. Transfer to a jar, cover tightly, and refrigerate. The applesauce will keep for at least 5 days in the refrigerator in a tightly sealed container. Makes about 2½ cups.

KIDS' STEPS Kids can wash and peel the apples and then transfer the finished sauce to a jar.

FUN FACTS
A Cook's Guide to Supermarket Apples

McIntosh: Named for Ontario farmer John McIntosh, who, in 1811, replanted some wild seeds. Ideal for sauce. A bit mushy for pies.

Red Delicious: Also known as the Hawkeye Delicious (it hails from Iowa) and the nation's best-seller. Sweet, juicy: the perfect snack. Not for baking.

Granny Smith: Tart and crisp, this Aussie baking and eating import discovered by grandma Anne Smith may be related to the crab apple.

(Royal) Gala: Queen Elizabeth II admired this one on a trip to New Zealand. Hence the name. It's royally versatile too, lovely baked or just off the tree.

Golden Delicious: Red's sister in name but not genetics. A West Virginia native, it holds firm in pies. Slices prettily too: the flesh doesn't brown.

Braeburn: Caramel's best buddy. When cooked, this New Zealand variety needs little if any sugar. It was discovered as a chance seedling in 1952.

Apple Dumplings

Wrapped in flaky pastry and basted in a cinnamon sauce, apple dumplings are in a league of their own and not that difficult to make. Just fill the apples with raisins, cut a few strategic snips in the rolled-out dough, and let your young chefs wrap things up.

PASTRY

1 3/4   cups flour

2   teaspoons sugar

3/4   teaspoon salt

10   tablespoons cold, unsalted butter, cut into 1/4-inch pieces

1/3   cup ice-cold water

FILLING AND SAUCE

5   or 6 small baking apples

3/4   cup dark raisins or currants

4   tablespoons cold butter

3/4   cup apple cider

3/4   cup water

1/2   cup sugar

1/8   teaspoon cinnamon

Pinch of nutmeg

1 Combine the flour, sugar, salt, and butter in a mixing bowl. Use a pastry blender to cut in the butter until it resembles coarse crumbs. Add the cold water and then mix the dough with your hands.

2 Turn the dough out onto a floured surface and pack it into a ball. Knead it once or twice, then dust it with flour and divide it into 5 or 6 pieces (one for each apple). Flatten each piece into a 1/2-inch-thick disk, wrap the disks individually in plastic wrap, and chill them for about 1 hour.

3 While the dough chills, core and peel the apples, leaving the lower third unpeeled.

4 Butter a large, shallow baking dish and heat the oven to 400°. Working with one piece of dough at a time (while keeping the others chilled), roll the pas-try into an 8-inch circle on a lightly floured surface, dusting your pin, if necessary, to keep it from sticking. Place an apple in the center of the circle. Fill the core loosely with raisins and press a tea-spoon-size dab of butter into the top.

5 Cut wedges about 2 inches long out of the pastry at the 12, 3, 6, and 9 o'clock positions, as shown, and reserve them.

6 Moisten all the dough edges with water. Fold one panel up over the apple, followed by the adjacent panel, then press them together to seal the seam. Repeat with the other panels.

7 To enclose the fruit (and form a stem) pinch together the excess pastry at the top of the apple. Cut leaves from the reserved pastry, brush the undersides with water, then press them onto the cov-ered apples. Arrange the dumplings in the baking dish and bake for 15 minutes.

8 While the dumplings bake, prepare the basting sauce. Combine the remain-ing butter (about 2 tablespoons), cider, water, sugar, cinnamon, and nutmeg in a medium saucepan and bring to a boil. Reduce the heat and simmer for 5 min-utes, stirring occasionally.

9 Baste the dumplings with some of the sauce, then pour the rest into the pan. Reduce the oven temperature to 375° and bake for another 30 to 45 minutes, bast-ing every 10 minutes. When the apples are tender (check with a toothpick), transfer the pan to a cooling rack. Serve warm or at room temperature.

KIDS' STEPS Kids can measure and mix the pastry, peel the apples, wrap the fruit in dough, and help baste the dumplings.

Berry Mint Toss

• •

Tossed with fresh mint, lemon juice, and honey, this strawberry treat makes for a quick snack or dessert that even a preschooler can help mix up.

- 2 pints strawberries
  Juice of half a lemon
- 10 to 15 fresh mint leaves
- 2 tablespoons honey

Rinse the berries in a colander, then pat them dry on a paper towel. Hull and slice them (younger kids can use a plastic knife).

In a serving bowl, toss the berries with the lemon juice. Mince the mint and add it and the honey to the bowl. Stir and let marinate for 30 minutes. Serves 4 to 6.

PREP TIME: 20 minutes

Ladybugs on a Stick

A true crowd pleaser, these luscious ladybugs are fun to bring into the classroom or to serve at a children's party.

INGREDIENTS
- 4 red grapes
- 8 trimmed wooden skewers
- 8 strawberries
- 40 mini chocolate chips
- 1 honeydew melon half

1 For each ladybug, push half of a red grape onto a trimmed wooden skewer for the head. Next, push on a hulled strawberry body and score the back to create wings.

2 For spots, use a toothpick to gently press mini chocolate chips, tips down, into the fruit. Arrange the skewers on a honeydew melon half. Makes 8 ladybugs.

KIDS' STEPS Kids can spear the grapes and strawberries on the skewers and press the chocolate chips into the fruit.

Fruit Flowers

Invite your child to plant these berry delicious flowers on his or her snack plate. It makes for a fun activity and healthful snack all in one.

STRAWBERRY FLOWER

- 1 kiwi slice
- 3 strawberries, sliced
  Red shoestring licorice
- 2 fresh mint leaves

RASPBERRY FLOWER

- 1 banana slice
- 10 raspberries
   Red shoestring licorice
- 2 fresh mint leaves

1 Set out a selection of sliced fruits and have your child create the sweet flowers.

2 For the flower centers, use a slice of banana or kiwi. Arrange raspberry or strawberry petals around it, then add a shoestring licorice stem with real mint leaves. Makes 2 flowers.

KIDS' STEPS Kids can create and decorate their own fruit flowers.

FUN FOOD

Frozen Fruit Pops

Instead of reaching into the freezer for your usual Popsicle, try one of these fruit pops. They're more fun because they have a unique shape, yummy taste, and no artificial flavors.

THE BEST FRUITS TO FREEZE: Banana halves, orange sections, whole strawberries without stems, mango spears, single grapes, and peeled kiwis. **HOW TO MAKE THEM:** Slide the fruit on a craft stick (use a toothpick for grapes), cover it with a plastic sandwich bag, secure it with a twist tie, and freeze for about 2 hours before serving. **TIP:** Freeze several pops per bag, unless the fruit is quite juicy (in which case the pops may stick together).

Mix-Your-Own Maple-Vanilla Yogurt

The homemade yogurt at right tastes just as good as the store-bought flavored kind, but has only a moderate amount of sweetening. And even toddlers can pitch in on this simple kitchen project.

INGREDIENTS

1 ½ cups plain yogurt

¼ cup real maple syrup

½ teaspoon vanilla extract

Strawberry jam (optional)

Mint leaves (optional)

1 Measure the yogurt into a medium-size bowl. Add the maple syrup and vanilla extract and mix until they disappear into the yogurt.

2 Spoon into small bowls. Let your kids decorate each serving with dabs of strawberry jam and a tiny mint leaf, if desired. Serves 4.

KIDS' STEPS Kids can stir in the maple syrup and vanilla extract, then decorate each serving.

FUN FOOD

Party Parfait

• • • • • • • • • • • • • • • • • • • •

A creative presentation makes an ordinary snack, like yogurt and fresh fruit, seem extraordinary. If you don't have parfait glasses, find other fancy glasses, preferably transparent ones so the kids can see the layers.

Start by putting a layer of plain or vanilla yogurt in the bottom of the glass. Next, add a layer of fresh fruit, then granola (or another favorite cereal). Spoon in more yogurt and add another layer of fruit and cereal. Top off with fresh fruit slices and a dollop of yogurt. Refrigerate until serving time.

Maple-Yogurt Fruit Dip

Whether you have toddlers or teens, this great dip can be your secret to getting them to eat a healthy serving of fruit.

INGREDIENTS

½ cup vanilla yogurt

1 ½ tablespoons maple syrup

½ teaspoon lemon juice

Strawberries, bananas, apples, or seedless red grapes

1 In a small bowl, stir together the yogurt, maple syrup, and lemon juice.

2 Cut the fruit and spear it on toothpicks to dip it in the sauce.

KIDS' STEPS Kids can mix the dip together and help cut up the fruit and spear it on toothpicks.

Strawberry-Yogurt Smoothies

For a nutritious and easy after-school snack, serve up a round of these fruity shakes. Customize your smoothies to suit your children's tastes (you can omit the banana, for example, and add blueberries in its place).

INGREDIENTS

- ½ pint strawberries
- 1 banana
- 2 8-ounce containers strawberry yogurt
- 1 cup milk

1 Wash and hull the strawberries, then pat them dry. Peel and slice the banana, then place all the fruit in a blender.

2 Add the yogurt to the blender, then pour in the milk. Blend until smooth and thoroughly combined, about 1 to 2 minutes.

3 For a creative presentation, have your child garnish each drink with a fruit kebab (a strawberry and banana slice threaded on a bamboo skewer) and a colorful plastic straw. Makes 32 ounces, or four 8-ounce shakes.

KIDS' STEPS Kids can wash, dry, and hull the strawberries and add the fruit to the blender.

Strawberry Smoothie Pops

The smoothie above freezes into tasty Popsicles that are fun to make and to eat.

INGREDIENTS

- 1 prepared Strawberry-Yogurt Smoothies recipe (above)
- Popsicle mold

1 Carefully pour the Strawberry-Yogurt Smoothies mixture into a plastic Popsicle mold. Freeze for 4 to 6 hours.

2 Dip the mold in warm water, then unmold the pops. Makes 6 to 8 pops.

KIDS' STEPS Kids can pour the mixture into the molds.

PREP TIME: **10 minutes**

Pineapple Crush

This smoothie, fresh and tropical, is an excellent source of vitamin C. Keep in mind that the riper the banana, the sweeter your shake.

INGREDIENTS

½ cup orange juice
½ cup pineapple juice
1 cup frozen pineapple chunks
½ frozen very ripe medium banana

1 Combine all the fruit in a blender.

2 Blend on high until slushy. Serves 2.

 KIDS' STEPS Kids can add the fruit to the blender.

PREP TIME: **10 minutes**

Purple Mango

Mango, one of the world's most popular fruits (and a vitamin C powerhouse), is finally getting its due stateside. Some grocery stores now sell it chopped and frozen, so you don't have to wrestle with cutting it fresh.

INGREDIENTS

1 cup pineapple juice
½ cup orange juice
1 cup frozen blueberries
1 cup cubed, frozen mango

1 Combine all ingredients in a blender.

2 Blend on high until slushy. Serves 2.

KIDS' STEPS Kids can measure the ingredients and push the button on the blender.

KITCHEN CRAFT
Silly Sippers

Getting your kids to drink plenty of beverages (or the smoothies at left) on a hot summer day can be a breeze if you serve them with decorated straws like the ones shown below.

To create a funny-face straw to use for your smoothies, simply cut an oval head from a piece of colored craft foam. Then cut out foam eyes, mouth, and hair (if desired) and glue the pieces onto the head. Use a hole punch to make an opening where the nose goes and push the end of a flexible plastic straw through it.

For flower straws, cut out a foam circle, then trim the edge to resemble petals. Punch a hole in the middle for the straw. Use the same method to add a second layer of petals or a colorful center.

PREP TIME: 20 minutes

Vegetable Flowers

Let your kids play with their food — and make the creative crudités at left. Once their flower is in bloom, they can dip the petals in the easy-to-mix ranch dip at right.

INGREDIENTS

Assorted vegetables, such as radish slices, fresh spinach leaves, cucumber rounds, cherry tomatoes, celery sticks, and baby carrots

DIRECTIONS

Set out vegetables and let your kids design their own flowers (there is no right or wrong way of doing this). We used radish slices and cucumber rounds for petals, cherry tomatoes for flower centers, celery sticks for stems, spinach for leaves, and baby carrots for grass.

KIDS' STEPS Kids can design the veggie flowers and help measure and mix up the ranch dip.

PREP TIME: 15 minutes

Rancher's Delight

Little cowpokes will get a kick out of constructing these clever cowboy boot crudités.

INGREDIENTS

Assorted vegetables, such as cucumber rounds, cherry tomatoes, peppers (yellow, green, and red), celery sticks, mushrooms, cauliflower, baby carrots

Ranch dip (see right)

DIRECTIONS

Form the outline of a cowboy boot using green pepper slices, then fill in with rows of baby carrots, cherry tomatoes, cucumber slices, celery, mushrooms, and cauliflower. As a finishing touch, add a bell pepper toe and spur. Serve with the ranch dip at right.

KIDS' STEPS Kids can lay out the boot design and help measure and mix up the ranch dip.

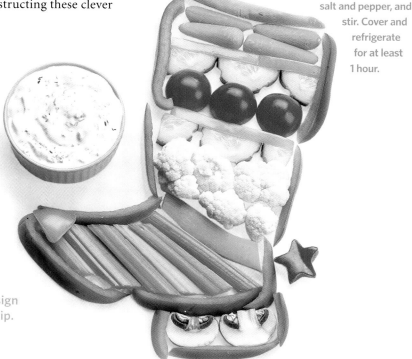

Healthy Hummus Dip

Made from chickpeas and tahini (a sesame seed paste) this classic Middle Eastern spread makes a nutritious appetizer or sandwich filling.

KIDS' STEPS Kids can measure the ingredients and press the buttons on the food processor.

INGREDIENTS

1   19-ounce can chickpeas
1   garlic clove
¼   cup tahini
2   to 3 tablespoons lemon juice, to taste
2   tablespoons olive oil
¼   teaspoon cumin (optional)

1 Drain the chickpeas in a colander, then rinse them thoroughly in cold water to rinse away the high-sodium liquid they are packed in. Set aside.

2 Peel the garlic clove and place it in a food processor fitted with a metal blade. Process until the garlic is chopped (you may need to scrape the inside of the bowl a few times to ensure the garlic is finely minced).

3 Add the rinsed chickpeas to the food processor, then add the tahini, lemon juice, olive oil, and cumin, if desired. Process for 1 minute or until smooth. Makes 2 cups.

PREP TIME: 5 minutes   BAKING TIME: about 5 minutes

Easy Pita Chips

These healthful chips are easy for kids to make and are the perfect "cracker" for the Healthy Hummus Dip above.

INGREDIENTS

Pita bread
Olive oil (optional)

KIDS' STEPS Kids can pull apart the wedges of pita bread and brush with olive oil.

1 Heat the oven to 375°. Cut a sandwich-size pita into sixths. Separate the top and bottom of each wedge.

2 Lay the wedges on a baking sheet, brush with olive oil (if you like) and bake until crisp and slightly brown, about 5 minutes.

PREP TIME: 20 minutes

Cherry Tomato and Cucumber Bites

Kids will love squirting cream cheese through a pastry bag and into hollowed-out cherry tomatoes and cucumber slices to make this snack. Use room-temperature cream cheese for best results.

INGREDIENTS

- 1 package (8 ounces) cream cheese, softened
- ¼ cup finely chopped basil leaves
- 1 garlic clove, crushed
- 1 tablespoon grated Parmesan (optional)
  Cucumbers and cherry tomatoes
  Fresh dill (optional)

1 In a small mixing bowl, stir the cream cheese until smooth. Add the chopped basil, garlic, and Parmesan (if desired) and stir until thoroughly combined. Set aside.

2 Score the sides of a cucumber with a zester, potato peeler, or knife. Then, cut the cucumber into 1-inch-thick rounds and scoop out the seeds with a melon baller. Slice off the tops of the cherry tomatoes with a serrated knife and scoop out the insides with the baller.

3 Fill a pastry bag, fitted with a star tip, with the cream cheese. If you don't have a pastry bag, fill a sealable freezer bag and snip off a small hole in the corner.

4 Squirt the cream cheese into the vegetables, as shown below. Garnish with sprigs of fresh dill and serve immediately. Makes 1 cup of flavored cream cheese, enough to fill 30 vegetables.

FUN FOOD
Mr. Tomato Head
. . . .

Bright and cheerful, these pea-brained fellows may actually tempt your child to eat vegetables. With a serrated knife (parents only), slice the top off a small tomato or cherry tomato; reserve the top for the hat. Scoop out the inside with a teaspoon or melon baller, turn the tomato upside down to drain, then fill with peas.

Your child can use cream cheese to glue on a pair of canned black-bean eyes, yellow-pepper nose, and a celery grin. Put his hat back on, and he's ready to paint the town red.

KIDS' STEPS Kids can stir the herbs into the cream cheese and squeeze the mix into the hollowed-out vegetables.

COOKING BASICS
Guacamole
. . . .

This traditional Mexican dip is so tasty that kids would never guess it's also packed with vitamins and minerals. In fact, one cup of avocado has more potassium than an equal serving of bananas.

3	ripe avocados
	Juice of 1 lime
1/2	small onion, chopped
1	crushed garlic clove
1/2	teaspoon pepper
1/2	teaspoon salt
1/2	cup salsa (optional)

Peel and chop the avocados and place the pieces in a small mixing bowl. (Reserve one of the avocado pits.) Using a fork, mash the avocados until you have a creamy mixture. Stir in the fresh lime juice. Add the onion, garlic, pepper, and salt and mix well. Add the salsa to the avocado mixture if you want to give the guacamole a little kick.

Guacamole is best served within an hour or so of making it, since it browns quickly. Put the avocado pit in the guacamole to slow this process. Makes about 2 cups.

PREP TIME: **20 minutes**   CHILLING TIME: **30 minutes**

Farm-Stand Salsa

Known also as pico de gallo or salsa fresca, this is one of the simplest salsas to make. And it tastes great scooped up with your favorite tortilla chips or nachos.

INGREDIENTS

2	large ripe tomatoes
4	scallions
1	mild green chili or 1 small green bell pepper
1/4	to 1/2 cup lightly packed cilantro leaves
1/2	lime
	Salt to taste

1 Core the tomatoes, then cut them crosswise into 1/4-inch-thick slices. Finely dice the slices and transfer them to a medium-size bowl.

2 Wash the scallions well, then trim off the trailing strands of the root end, as well as any sections that don't look or feel crisp. Slice thinly, then mix with the tomatoes.

3 Slice open the chili or green pepper and scrape away any seeds. Dice the chili or pepper and add it to the tomatoes. (Note: if using a chili, wash your hands well afterward, as the chili's oil can irritate your skin.) Finely chop the cilantro and stir it into the salsa.

4 Squeeze the juice from the lime into the salsa and stir. Add a generous pinch of salt and stir again. Cover and chill for 30 minutes.

5 Just before serving, sample a spoonful and add more lime juice and salt if needed. Makes about 2 cups.

KIDS' STEPS Kids can help dice the tomato slices with a plastic knife and squeeze the lime into the salsa.

"For fun, I sometimes include a Mystery Treat in my son's lunch. It might be a familiar snack, like chocolate chips, a new food he has never tried, such as pistachios, or something just a little unusual, like gummy sharks.

"I wrap the treat in aluminum foil to disguise it and attach a clue to the outside, so Trent, age ten, can try to guess what the treat is before he opens it. The Mystery Treats have become a lunchtime hit with Trent and his friends."

— *Jill Hibbard*
Interlochen, Michigan

PREP TIME: **10 minutes**   COOKING TIME: **about 10 minutes**

Tortilla Chip Strips

Instead of your kids reaching for a bag of store-bought tortilla chips, invite them to make a basket of these healthy baked snacks. They can cut the flour tortillas with scissors into fun strips — just right for dipping into salsa.

INGREDIENTS

6   large flour tortillas
    Vegetable oil cooking spray
    Salt

1 Heat the oven to 375°. Set out 1 or 2 baking sheets. Use kitchen scissors, a pizza cutter, or a knife to cut each tortilla into ¼-inch strips.

2 Spread the tortilla strips on the baking sheet in a single layer. The pieces can touch but should not overlap. Holding the can of cooking spray about 12 inches away, lightly spray the tortillas. Sprinkle with salt.

KIDS' STEPS Kids can cut the flour tortillas with kitchen scissors, a plastic pizza wheel, or cookie cutters.

3 Bake the strips for 3 minutes. Remove them from the oven and stir with tongs or a metal spatula, letting some bend and twist. Return them to the oven and bake for 4 to 5 minutes, until lightly browned. Cool on the sheet, then slide the strips into a bowl. Serves 4 to 6.

TORTILLA CHIP CRITTERS
Instead of cutting the tortillas into strips, cut out shapes with animal-shaped cookie cutters.

PREP TIME: **5 to 10 minutes**

Popcorn-Banana Munch Mix

If your kids are tired of gorp, here's a creative variation. Simply start with cheesy popcorn, then mix in your favorite healthy snack foods.

INGREDIENTS

- 3 cups cheese-flavored popcorn
- 1/2 to 1 cup banana chips, broken into small pieces
- 1 cup dry-roasted peanuts
- 1/2 to 1 cup sweetened, dried cranberries

1 Measure all the ingredients into a big bowl (you can substitute your family's favorite natural snack foods, if desired).

2 Stir well. Makes 5 to 6 cups.

 KIDS' STEPS Kids can measure and mix up the munch mix.

PREP TIME: **about 20 minutes**   COOKING TIME: **about 5 minutes**

Popcorn S'mores

This stovetop recipe adds popcorn to the original campfire version of s'mores and turns the familiar snack into an easy, portable treat.

INGREDIENTS

- 1 cup light brown sugar, firmly packed
- 1/2 cup butter
- 1/2 cup corn syrup
- 1/2 teaspoon baking soda
- 10 cups freshly popped popcorn, cooled (do not use air-popped corn, as the kernels are too delicate for the hot syrup)
- 1 (10 1/2-ounce) package mini marshmallows
- 2 cups mini graham cookies (we used Teddy Grahams)
- 1 cup chocolate chips

1 Combine the brown sugar, butter, and corn syrup in a medium saucepan and cook over high heat for 5 minutes (adults only; this mixture gets very hot). Remove from the heat and stir in the baking soda.

2 Combine the popcorn and the marshmallows in a large metal or heat-resistant glass bowl (not plastic; the heat could damage it). Drizzle the sugar mixture over the popcorn, then gently stir in the graham cookies and chocolate chips.

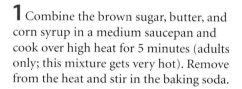

3 Let the mixture set until cool enough to handle, then, using buttered plastic sandwich bags on your hands, form the mixture into golf-ball-size balls. Store in an airtight container. Makes about 30.

KIDS' STEPS Kids can form the popcorn s'mores into balls using plastic sandwich bags as gloves.

Deviled Egg Boats

INGREDIENTS

- 12 hard-boiled eggs
- 2 teaspoons Dijon mustard
- 2 teaspoons vinegar (white or cider)
- ¼ to ½ cup mayonnaise
- 2 red, orange, yellow, or green bell peppers

   Paprika

A seaworthy take on the classic picnic food, these cleverly engineered eggs with a mustardy zip and colorful sails are sure to become an instant favorite with your crew.

1 Peel the eggs, then slice each one in half to make boats. Place the yolks in a medium-size bowl and mash them with a fork. Add the mustard and vinegar, then add the mayonnaise, stirring until the consistency is smooth but not soupy.

2 Next, make the sails. To do this, cut each pepper into 1-inch-wide strips, then cut the strips into 1-inch squares and slice each square in half diagonally.

3 Fill the egg-white halves with the yolk mixture. Stick the sail upright into the filling and sprinkle with paprika. Makes 2 dozen.

KIDS' STEPS Kids can peel the eggs, mash the yolk mixture, and put the pepper sails on.

PREP TIME: about 10 minutes

Shipshape Snack

Launch a fleet of edible sailboats for a nutritional snack your kids will sail right through.

INGREDIENTS

- Red pepper
- Tuna or egg salad
- Thin pretzel stick
- Cheese slice
- Cream cheese (dab)
- Red pepper flag

1 Cut a red pepper in half lengthwise (or into quarters for lighter fare) and remove the seeds.

2 Fill each pepper boat with lunchtime cargo, such as tuna or egg salad. Sink a thin pretzel stick mast into the center of the boat, then add 2 triangular pieces of cheese for sails.

3 Use a dab of cream cheese to fix a small red pepper flag to the top of the mast.

FUN FOOD
Hard-Boiled Egg Mice

. . . .

With chive tails, radish ears, and olive eyes, hard-boiled eggs get transformed into whimsical mice (that like to be served wedges of cheese, please).

To make each mouse, slice off a bit of the bottom of a peeled, hard-boiled egg so it can sit flat on a plate as shown. Then slice tiny black olive eyes and radish ears. Make small slits in the egg for the eyes and ears and push in the olives and radishes as shown. Add a chive tail and serve with a tiny wedge of Swiss cheese.

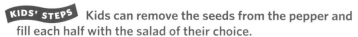

KIDS' STEPS Kids can remove the seeds from the pepper and fill each half with the salad of their choice.

PREP TIME: 10 minutes   **BAKING TIME:** about 10 minutes

Pizza Mummies

Disguises aren't just for Halloween. Surprise your family with these dressed-up, spooky-looking snacks any time of year.

INGREDIENTS

Pizza sauce

English muffins

Black olives

Scallions

Red or green pepper

Cheese sticks or slices

1 Heat the oven to 350°. For each mummy, spread a tablespoon of pizza sauce onto half of an English muffin (toast it first, if you like).

2 Set olive slices in place for eyes and add round slices of green onion or bits of red or green pepper for pupils.

3 Lay strips of cheese (we used a pulled-apart cheese stick) across the muffin for the mummy's wrappings.

4 Bake for about 10 minutes, or until the cheese is melted and the muffin is toasty.

KIDS' STEPS Kids can spoon the pizza sauce on the English muffins and make the mummy faces with the cheese and vegetables.

PREP TIME: 10 minutes   **BAKING TIME:** about 20 to 25 minutes

Pizza Dippers

Bread sticks and dip make a fun and tasty pizza substitute. Whichever pizza toppings your family prefers — pepperoni, cheese, veggies — this versatile dip recipe lets you enjoy all the great flavors of a classic pie without making a crust.

INGREDIENTS

- 8 ounces ricotta cheese
- 1 cup mayonnaise
- ¼ cup grated Parmesan cheese
- 1 teaspoon Italian seasoning
- ½ teaspoon garlic powder
- 1½ cups shredded mozzarella cheese

  Chopped pizza toppings, such as tomatoes, red or green peppers, mushrooms, pepperoni, or cooked sausage

1 Heat the oven to 350°. Combine the ricotta cheese, mayonnaise, Parmesan cheese, Italian seasoning, and garlic powder in a medium bowl. Stir in 1 cup of the mozzarella cheese. Mix well.

2 Spoon the mixture into six 6-ounce ramekins, then sprinkle each one with the remaining ½ cup of mozzarella.

3 Place the ramekins on a cookie sheet and bake until the dips are heated through and the tops are lightly browned, about 20 to 25 minutes.

4 Garnish each dish with the chopped pizza toppings. Serve warm with bread sticks, crackers, or pita chips. Serves 6.

KIDS' STEPS Kids can measure and mix the ingredients and garnish the dishes with toppings.

Sweet Hearts

This colorful new twist on a classic treat is a great gift for your children to give on Valentine's Day to anyone they're sweet on.

INGREDIENTS

Cooking spray

¼   cup (½ stick) butter

4   cups mini marshmallows

Red food coloring

6   cups crisped rice cereal

Heart-shaped cookie cutter

Plastic bags

Yarn

1 Lightly coat a 13- by 9-inch baking pan with cooking spray and set it aside.

2 Melt the butter in a large pot over low heat. Add the marshmallows, stirring them continuously until they melt. Remove the pan from the heat and stir in drops of red food coloring until you achieve your desired shade.

3 Add the cereal, stirring until it is all evenly coated with the marshmallow. Spoon the mixture onto the baking sheet and smooth it out to an even thickness.

4 While the mixture is still warm, cut out hearts with the cookie cutter. Once cooled, place each in a clear plastic bag. Tie on a yarn bow, and it's ready for giving. Makes five 5-inch hearts.

KIDS' STEPS Older kids can mix the marshmallows and add the food coloring. Younger kids can use the cookie cutter to make the hearts. Both can help package the treats.

PREP TIME: 20 minutes   **COOKING TIME:** 15 minutes

Mock Sushi

There's definitely something fishy about these Japanese-style rolls. The rice filling is crispy, the wraps are fruity, and your kids will love them — no fooling!

INGREDIENTS

	Cooking spray
1/4	cup (1/2 stick) butter
4	cups mini marshmallows
6	cups crisped rice cereal
	Gummy worms
	Fruit Roll-Ups

1 Lightly coat a 12- by 17-inch baking sheet with the cooking spray.

2 Melt the butter in a 2-quart saucepan over medium heat. Add the marshmallows and stir until smooth. Remove the mixture from the heat and stir in the cereal until it's evenly coated.

3 Turn the baking sheet so that the shorter ends are at the top and bottom, then press the marshmallow mixture onto the sheet, distributing it evenly.

4 Starting at one side an inch up from the lower edge, place gummy worms atop the mixture end to end in a horizontal line. Gently roll the lower edge of the marshmallow mixture over the gummy worms. Then stop and cut the log away from the rest of the mixture. Use the same method to form 4 more logs. Slice each log into 1-inch-thick "sushi" rolls and wrap them individually with strips of Fruit Roll-Ups. Makes 4 to 5 dozen.

KIDS' STEPS   Kids can press the marshmallow mixture onto the baking sheet, line up the gummy worms, and roll up the "sushi."

FUN FOOD
Crispy Rice Pops

For a snack you can sell at a bake sale, try these crunchy, chocolaty lollipops. *FamilyFun* reader Shelley Kotulka came up with this sweet idea for a craft fair in Wind Gap, Pennsylvania, and her treats sold out in no time.

Prepare the marshmallow-cereal treat as directed in step 2 of the Mock Sushi recipe at left.

Let the mixture cool until it's warm but comfortable to handle with your fingers. Lightly butter your hands, then shape the treats into 12 balls. Push a Popsicle stick into each one, then set them aside to cool.

While the pops are cooling, melt 1 1/2 cups of white or semisweet chocolate in a metal bowl set over a pan of hot, but not boiling, water. Dip the tops of the marshmallow treats into the chocolate and add sprinkles.

Set the lollipops on a waxed paper-lined tray. Once the chocolate has hardened, wrap the treats in plastic and tie with a ribbon.

CHAPTER FOUR

SOUPS

Stir up something good with a hearty soup or stew

SOUPS AND STEWS ARE QUINTESSENTIAL COMFORT FOODS. Wholesome, nourishing, and aromatic, they warm body and soul. Serve one up as a savory opener or pair it with a basket of biscuits, bread, or popovers for a simple and satisfying meal. Soups also freeze and reheat easily, so you can cook a big batch on a lazy Sunday and set it aside for quick weekday suppers. Best of all, because they invite experimentation and are so forgiving of mistakes, soups and stews are the perfect training ground for budding young cooks. Try these suggestions with yours.

LET KIDS BE SOUP SOUS CHEFS. Soup making is a cooking technique that can grow as your kids do. Most soup recipes require a variety of skills you can teach your kids. Under supervision, they can chop vegetables with a plastic or paring knife, snip fresh herbs with scissors, or gently stir the hot soup on the stove.

USE RAMEN AS A BASE. For a beginner recipe, have your kids prepare ramen soup mix. Then they can add their favorite vegetables, such as snap peas or a diced tomato.

KEEP IT SEPARATE. Keep parts of the soup you're not sure your kids will like in a separate serving dish and have them try a bite before adding it (or not) to their simpler version.

LOOK OUT FOR LEFTOVERS. All sorts of things can go into soups — vegetables, meatballs, leftover pasta or rice, or that last bit of grilled chicken. Scout possibilities and stash them in the freezer until assembly time.

STOCK UP ON CHICKEN STOCK. The basis of many of the soups in this chapter is broth. Sample a few brands to find the one that suits your family's taste the best, then buy enough to keep on hand for soup days at home.

SHARE YOUR FAVORITES. *FamilyFun* reader Vicki Hodges chases away the cold in Hotchkiss, Colorado, each winter by hosting a soup potluck for her friends. Guests bring a pot of soup, along with crackers or biscuits, to share.

Starry, Starry Soup

Want to warm up your family on a nippy day? Pull together a batch of this steaming chicken soup.

INGREDIENTS

1   or 2 medium carrots

4   cups chicken broth

    Dash of sage or Bell's Seasoning

¼   cup mini star-shaped pasta or egg pastina

¾   cup chopped, cooked chicken

    Salt and pepper to taste

1 Scrub the carrots with a vegetable brush, then cut them into long, diagonal ¼-inch slices. Use an aspic cutter to cut star shapes out of the carrot slices, and set them aside.

2 In a medium pot, bring the broth to a simmer over medium heat. Stir in the sage or Bell's Seasoning and carrot stars and simmer until the carrots are tender, about 10 minutes more. Add the pasta and chicken. Continue cooking for another few minutes, stirring occasionally, just until the pasta is done. Makes 4 servings.

KIDS' STEPS   Younger kids can scrub the carrots clean. Older kids can cut the stars out of the vegetables.

· ·

TIP: To make stars for your soup, cut the carrots into long diagonal slices about ¼ inch thick. Use a very small cookie cutter or an aspic cutter to cut stars from the slices.

Tortilla Soup

Cooked up by *FamilyFun* reader Bonnie Alexander of Dallas, this colorful soup
turns dinner into a Mexican fiesta. Her choose-your-own-add-ins approach
produces a family meal that can be different every time it's served.

INGREDIENTS

2   quarts chicken broth

2   cups corn kernels

3   Roma tomatoes, chopped

4   tablespoons salsa

2   boneless chicken breasts

4   tablespoons soy sauce

10 corn tortillas

   Oil for frying

1   ripe avocado

1   tablespoon lemon juice

2   cups grated Monterey Jack cheese

1/2 bunch cilantro

1 In a large soup pot, mix the broth, corn, tomatoes, and salsa. Bring to a boil, cover, and simmer.

2 Marinate the chicken in the soy sauce for at least 15 minutes, and up to an hour.

3 Cut the tortillas into 1-inch strips. Fry five strips at a time in 1 inch of heated oil until golden brown. Drain the strips well on paper towels and store them in a warm oven.

4 Grill or sauté the chicken, slice it into strips, and set it aside, covered.

5 Cube the avocado and sprinkle with lemon juice. Place the remaining toppings in bowls on the table.

6 Each diner can fill a soup bowl with chicken, tortilla strips, avocado, and/or cheese, then ladle on the hot broth. Makes 6 to 8 servings.

KIDS' STEPS Kids can squeeze lemon juice on the avocado cubes and put the add-ins in bowls.

Egg Drop Soup

Perhaps the best part of this simple-to-make soup is perfecting your "drop" technique. You can choose to cook your eggs into skinny strands, thicker ribbons, or tiny shreds.

INGREDIENTS

    4   cups chicken broth
    3   tablespoons water
    1   tablespoon cornstarch
    1   egg, lightly beaten
  10   to 12 fresh snow peas
    1   green onion, finely sliced
  ¼   cup finely chopped ham (optional)

1 Bring the chicken broth to a simmer in a 2½- to 3-quart saucepan over medium-high heat.

2 In a separate bowl, combine the water and cornstarch, then stir the cornstarch mixture into the simmering broth. Bring the broth to a boil, then remove it from the heat.

3 Slowly pour in the egg and gently stir it with a fork in one direction only, stirring slowly for long strands of egg, more rapidly for thinner shreds.

4 Add the snow peas and the green onion, then the ham, if desired. Let the soup stand for a few minutes before serving. Makes 4 servings.

KIDS' STEPS Younger kids can mix the water and cornstarch together. Older kids can "drop" the beaten egg into the soup.

PREP TIME: 25 minutes   COOKING TIME: 20 minutes

Wonton Soup

The noodle-and-meat dumplings in this soup make it a fun and tasty starter for just about any meal. If you end up with extra wonton filling, simply freeze it for later or sauté it on the side and add it to individual bowls of soup.

INGREDIENTS

- ½   pound ground pork or ground beef
- 2   scallions, finely chopped
- 1   garlic clove, minced
- 1   tablespoon stir-fry sauce
-     Dashes of salt and pepper
- 12   to 16 wonton wrappers
- 6½   cups chicken broth
- 1½   cups very thinly sliced bok choy
- 1   medium carrot, peeled and shredded
- ½   teaspoon toasted sesame oil

1 Combine the meat, scallions, garlic, and stir-fry sauce in a medium mixing bowl. Lightly salt and pepper the ingredients. With clean hands or a spoon, mix the filling together.

2 Set the wonton wrappers on a flat work surface and spoon ½ tablespoon of the filling onto the center of each one. Shape and fold the wontons (see directions at right), then transfer them to a wax paper-lined cookie sheet.

3 Bring a medium pot of water to a boil. Meanwhile, combine the chicken broth, bok choy, carrot, and sesame oil in a medium saucepan. Salt to taste. Cover the pan and bring to a low boil. Reduce the heat and simmer for 2 to 3 minutes, until the bok choy is tender, then turn off the heat.

4 By now, the water in the first pot should have come to a boil. Add 1 teaspoon of salt. Then use a slotted spoon to carefully drop in the wontons, one at a time. Keep the water at a low boil until the filling is cooked, about 6 to 7 minutes. With the slotted spoon, carefully lift the wontons from the water and place several in each soup bowl.

5 Quickly reheat the chicken broth and ladle some over the wontons in each bowl. Makes 6 servings.

KIDS' STEPS Kids can mix the meat filling together, spoon it onto the wonton wrappers, and fold up the wrappers.

COOKING BASICS
Folding Wontons

Here's a simple method for folding wontons. Lay each noodle wrapper flat on a countertop and spoon the filling onto the center of the square. Use a pastry brush or your fingers to moisten the noodle edges with water. Then fold the wrapper in half diagonally, firmly pinching the edges to seal in the filling.

PREP TIME: **about 15 minutes**   COOKING TIME: **about 30 minutes**

Corn and Potato Chowder

This rich, creamy chowder is the perfect comfort food — reassuring, full-bodied, and delicious. And it's easier to make than a lot of cream soups because you don't have to puree anything.

INGREDIENTS

- 2 tablespoons butter
- 1 large onion, finely chopped
- 1 rib celery, finely chopped
- 5 1/2 cups chicken stock
- 1 1/2 cups corn kernels
- 1 large all-purpose potato, peeled and diced
- 1/2 to 3/4 teaspoon salt, to taste
- 1 cup heavy cream
- 3 tablespoons flour
- Black pepper to taste
- Fresh, chopped dill or parsley for garnish

1 Melt the butter in a large saucepan or medium soup pot. Stir in the onion and celery. Partially cover the pan and cook the vegetables over moderate heat for 10 minutes, stirring occasionally.

2 Add the chicken stock, corn, potato, and salt and bring the mixture to a low boil. Lower the heat, cover the pot, and simmer until the potatoes are just tender, about 7 minutes.

3 In a small bowl, whisk together the cream and flour, then stir it into the soup with the pepper. Bring the soup back to a low boil, then reduce the heat and simmer for about 8 minutes. Garnish with herbs. Makes 6 servings.

KIDS' STEPS Older kids can peel the potatoes, mix the cream and flour together, and top the bowls of soup with the herbs.

PREP TIME: **10 minutes**   COOKING TIME: **1 hour**

Potato Leek Soup

The light flavors of potatoes and leeks combine in this refreshing white soup. It is surprisingly easy to make — just be sure you wash the leeks thoroughly to remove any sand.

INGREDIENTS

- 5 cups peeled, chopped all-purpose potatoes
- 3 cups thinly sliced leeks (use the white and 2 inches of the green)
- 1 2/3 cups chicken broth
- 5 cups water
- 1 teaspoon salt
- 1/2 teaspoon white pepper
- 1/2 cup heavy cream
- Chopped chives (optional)

1 In a soup pot, add the potatoes, leeks, broth, water, salt, and pepper, and simmer for 1 hour.

2 In batches, puree the soup and pour it into a large bowl. Stir in the cream. Serve warm or cold. Makes 6 to 8 servings.

KIDS' STEPS Kids can peel the potatoes and stir the cream into the pureed soup.

Tortellini Vegetable Soup

Packed with tortellini, this hearty soup is popular with kids and nutritious enough to serve as a main dish.

INGREDIENTS

2	tablespoons olive oil
1	medium onion, chopped
1	small zucchini, diced
1	medium carrot, peeled and diced
5 1/2	cups chicken stock
1	teaspoon dried basil (more if fresh)
1	bay leaf
1/2	cup canned crushed tomatoes
1/2	teaspoon salt
8	to 9 ounces fresh or frozen tortellini (cheese or meat)
2	to 3 tablespoons chopped fresh parsley
	Black pepper to taste

1 Heat the olive oil in a medium soup pot or large saucepan. Add the onion, zucchini, and carrot. Sauté over moderate heat, stirring often, until the onion is soft and translucent, about 8 to 10 minutes.

2 Add the stock, basil, bay leaf, tomatoes, and salt to the pot. Increase the heat and bring the mixture to a low boil.

3 Add the tortellini and bring the soup back to a low boil. Cook it for 2 minutes, then reduce the heat and let it simmer for 5 to 6 minutes longer. Gently stir in the parsley and pepper during the last minute or so. Makes about 5 servings.

KIDS' STEPS Kids can wash and peel the vegetables, measure the herbs and spices, and help add the ingredients to the pot.

PREP TIME: 30 minutes   **COOKING TIME:** 45 minutes

Sweet Sausage Minestrone

This everything-but-the-kitchen-sink soup has something for everyone. Make it on a weekend afternoon; the delicious smell will fill the house.

INGREDIENTS

1	large onion, chopped
1	tablespoon olive oil
1	red bell pepper, chopped
1	green bell pepper, chopped
1	garlic clove, crushed
1	13-ounce can beef broth
3	cups water
1	28-ounce can crushed tomatoes
2	cups coarsely chopped cabbage
6	Italian sweet sausages (about 1 pound)
1	tablespoon basil
1	tablespoon oregano
1	teaspoon salt
1/4	teaspoon pepper
1	15-ounce can cannellini beans, drained
1/2	cup sliced olives
1	can (8 1/2 ounces) artichoke hearts
1	1-pound package fresh tortellini
	Chopped fresh parsley
	Grated Parmesan cheese

1 In a soup pot, sauté the onion in the oil until translucent. Add the red and green peppers and the garlic and sauté for 5 minutes.

2 Add the broth, water, tomatoes, cabbage, sausages, basil, oregano, salt, and pepper. Bring to a boil, then cook over medium-low heat for 20 minutes.

3 Remove the sausages, cut them into ½-inch rounds, and return them to the pot. Add the beans, olives, and artichoke hearts and cook for 5 minutes.

4 Just before serving, add the tortellini and cook in the soup until al dente. Garnish with the fresh parsley and Parmesan cheese. Makes 8 to 10 servings.

KIDS' STEPS Older kids can chop the vegetables. Younger kids can help add the ingredients to the soup pot.

FOOD FOR THOUGHT
Soup Stories

While your soup is simmering, read one of these wonderful stories to your child.

In *Mean Soup* by Betsy Everit (Harcourt Brace & Co.), Horace learns soup soothes his anger.

Growing Vegetable Soup by Lois Ehlert (Harcourt Brace Jovanovich) tells of a family who farm the vegetables they use to make their soup.

Marisa makes dumplings to celebrate a new year in *Dumpling Soup* by Jama Kim Rattigan (Little, Brown).

Traveling soldiers trick the inhabitants of a village into combining their bits of food to make a meal for all in *Stone Soup* by Marcia Brown (Simon & Schuster).

Meatball Alphabet Soup

This rich alphabet and mini meatball soup will warm up any cold winter day.

MEATBALLS

- ½ cup dried bread crumbs
- ½ cup grated Parmesan cheese
- 2 tablespoons minced onion
- 1 garlic clove, minced
- 2 tablespoons minced, fresh parsley
- 2 teaspoons dried basil
- ½ teaspoon salt
- ½ teaspoon pepper
- 1 large egg, lightly beaten
- 1 pound ground beef
   Oil or cooking spray for the pan

SOUP

- 2 tablespoons olive oil
- 1 small onion, finely chopped
- 1 rib celery, finely chopped
- 1 garlic clove, minced
- 5 cups chicken stock
- 1 cup crushed canned tomatoes in puree
- 1 teaspoon Italian seasoning
- ½ teaspoon salt
   Pepper to taste
- ⅓ cup alphabet pasta, dry

1 To make the meatballs, combine the bread crumbs, Parmesan cheese, onion, garlic, herbs, and spices in a large mixing bowl. Use a fork to mix in the egg, then add the ground beef, mixing well with your hands. Shape the mixture into 1-inch balls (you should get about 4 dozen).

2 Heat a frying pan coated with oil or cooking spray. Place the meatballs in the pan and cook them over medium-low heat for 8 to 10 minutes, turning them often so they brown evenly, until the centers are only slightly pink. (If you have more meatballs than you want to use, freeze the extras and toss them into your next pot of soup.)

3 To make the soup, heat the oil in a medium soup pot. Add the onion, celery, and garlic. Partially cover the pot and cook the vegetables over moderate heat for 8 to 10 minutes, stirring occasionally.

4 Add the chicken stock, tomatoes, Italian seasoning, salt, and pepper. Bring the soup to a simmer over medium-low heat, then add the pasta and simmer gently until the pasta is almost cooked. Transfer the meatballs to the pot and simmer until they are fully cooked, about 3 minutes more. Serves 6.

KIDS' STEPS Kids can measure the spices for the soup and help make the meatballs.

PREP TIME: about 10 minutes   **COOKING TIME:** about 15 minutes

Quick Tomato Soup

A classic kid favorite, this tomato soup recipe is a cinch for young hands to help make and boasts a start-to-finish time of less than 30 minutes.

INGREDIENTS

2   tablespoons olive oil or butter
1   cup minced onion
2   garlic cloves, crushed
½   teaspoon salt
1   can (28 ounces) whole, peeled tomatoes
1   cup milk
     Salt and pepper to taste
     Fresh basil or dill (optional)

1 Heat the olive oil or butter in a medium saucepan. Add the onion, garlic, and ½ teaspoon salt. Cook and stir over medium-low heat for about 10 minutes, or until the onions become very soft.

2 Place the tomatoes and their juice into a food processor or blender. Add the cooked onions and garlic and puree until smooth.

3 Pour the pureed mixture into a saucepan. Heat it slowly, stirring occasionally. When it's warm, drizzle in the milk.

4 Ladle the soup into serving bowls. If desired, add a few shakes of salt and pepper to taste. Stir in fresh dill or basil, if you like. Makes 4 servings.

KIDS' STEPS   Kids can measure the ingredients into the food processor or blender.

FOOD FOR THOUGHT
Soup Rules

Serving soup and bread for supper can be a prime — and appetizing — opportunity to teach your kids some basic table etiquette. When it comes to eating these foods by the book, here's what Judith Ré, an author and teacher of table manners, has to say.

EAT SOUP LIKE CLOCKWORK
Imagine that the part of your soup bowl closest to your chest is at 6 o'clock and the part farthest away is at 12. Fill your spoon by skimming it across the surface from 6 to 12. Raise your spoon and gently lean into it; don't drop your head down to your spoon like you're bobbing for apples.

MAKE IT BITE SIZE
What if you find an oversize piece of broccoli in your soup? Simply use your spoon to push it against the side of your bowl, then slice it with your spoon — and steady your bowl so it doesn't land in someone else's lap.

KEEP IT QUIET
Don't clank your spoon around in the bowl. To get those last drops, carefully tilt the bowl away from you so the soup puddles in one spot, then spoon it up.

DON'T BE A BREAD HOG
Sharing bread symbolizes our connections to those around us, so it involves a measure of etiquette and respect. The person nearest the bread basket passes it, always to the right. Never shake your head or hand if you're not interested. Accept the basket graciously and keep passing it. If someone asks for the bread basket, it's a no-no to pilfer from it first.

PREP TIME: 5 minutes   COOKING TIME: 30 minutes

Black Bean Soup

This filling soup at left can be whipped up in a dash and has a mildly spiced flavor, thanks to salsa in the mix. It reheats nicely too, so you might want to double the batch and freeze what's left for another night.

INGREDIENTS

- 1 cup salsa
- 2 cans (15 ½ ounces each) black beans, drained and rinsed
- 2 cups chicken broth
- 1 teaspoon lime juice
- 2 tablespoons chopped fresh cilantro
   Sour cream (optional)

 Kids can measure the ingredients and add them to the pot.

1 Heat the salsa in a large saucepan over medium heat, stirring often, for about 5 minutes. Stir in the beans and broth. Bring the mixture to a boil, then lower the heat and simmer the soup, covered, for 15 minutes.

2 Let the soup cool slightly, then ladle half of it into a food processor or blender and puree it. Return the pureed soup to the pot. Stir in the lime juice and chopped cilantro and heat the mixture through. Top each bowl with a dollop of sour cream, if desired. Makes 4 servings.

MY GREAT IDEA
Cool Peas

"My daughters, Becca, age three, and Maggie, two, love to eat soup. One day when I was caught without ice cubes to cool it down, I grabbed a handful of frozen peas instead. Not only did the soup cool quickly, but the peas were thawed and ready to eat. The girls thought the whole experiment was cool, and I loved that we'd made the soup even healthier. We've since added frozen corn, carrots, and green beans too. There are so many options!"

— *Cady Kilpeck*
Gansevoort, New York

PREP TIME: 15 minutes   COOKING TIME: about 1 hour

Split Pea Soup

On winter weekends, fill your home with the aroma of this hearty vegetarian soup.

INGREDIENTS

- 2 tablespoons olive oil
- 1 ½ cups chopped onions
- 3 carrots, peeled and diced
- 1 crushed garlic clove
- 2 cups split peas, rinsed
- 5 cups water
- 1 ⅔ cups vegetable or chicken broth
- 1 tablespoon dill or thyme
   Salt and pepper to taste
   Chopped fresh parsley

1 In a soup pot, sauté the onions, carrots, and garlic in the oil until the onions are translucent. Add the split peas along with the water, broth, and dill or thyme.

2 Simmer the split peas for about 1 hour in a covered pot until tender/mushy, stirring three to four times. Add more water or broth if the soup is too thick. Season with salt and pepper and garnish with parsley. Serves 6 to 8.

KIDS' STEPS Kids can rinse the peas and measure the ingredients.

Homemade Chili

Made with kidney beans, ground beef, and just the right amount of mild, warming spices, this is the ultimate, everyone-loves-it chili.

INGREDIENTS

2	15-ounce cans kidney beans (cooked)
4	tablespoons olive oil
1½	pounds ground chuck
2	medium onions, diced
1	medium green bell pepper, diced
2	or 3 garlic cloves, minced
1½	to 2 tablespoons mild chili powder
1	tablespoon cumin
1½	tablespoons flour
3	cups chicken or beef stock
1	teaspoon salt
1	28-ounce can crushed tomatoes in puree
1	tablespoon Worcestershire sauce
1	to 2 tablespoons steak sauce, such as A.1.
½	to 2 cups additional stock, tomato juice, or water, if needed
	Sour cream
	Cheddar cheese
	Jalapeño peppers (optional)

1 Drain the liquid from the canned beans, then rinse them in a colander.

2 Heat 1 tablespoon of the olive oil in a large skillet. Add half of the ground chuck and brown it. Using a slotted spoon, transfer the meat to a large soup pot or Dutch oven. Drain off all but 1 tablespoon of the fat in the skillet, then brown the remaining meat and add it to the pot. Discard all of the fat in the skillet.

3 Pour the remaining 3 tablespoons of olive oil into the empty skillet. Add the onions and peppers and sauté them over medium heat for 6 minutes, stirring often. Stir in the garlic and cook 2 minutes more.

4 Sprinkle the chili powder, cumin, and flour over the vegetables in the skillet and sauté for 1 minute more, stirring nonstop. Stir in 1 cup of the stock and cook for 1 minute. Transfer the contents of the skillet to the pot, along with the salt, crushed tomatoes, Worcestershire sauce, and steak sauce. Stir in the remaining 2 cups of stock and the beans.

5 Bring the chili to a low boil, stirring occasionally. Reduce the heat, cover, and simmer for 1 to 1½ hours, stirring occasionally. When done, the chili should be thick, but still somewhat soupy. If it starts to get too thick, add extra stock, tomato juice, or water. Serve with a dollop of sour cream, a sprinkle of Cheddar cheese, and, if desired, jalapeño peppers. Makes 8 or more servings.

KIDS' STEPS Kids can rinse the beans, measure the ingredients, and garnish the bowls of chili.

Butternut and Ham Bisque

INGREDIENTS

- 2 tablespoons butter
- 1 very large sweet onion, chopped
- 1/2 teaspoon chopped, dried rosemary leaves
- 2 cloves garlic, minced
- 5 cups peeled, diced butternut squash
- 1 cup peeled, diced all-purpose potatoes
- 5 cups chicken stock
- 1 teaspoon salt
- Black pepper to taste
- 1/2 cup light or heavy cream
- 1 1/2 cups diced cooked ham

This soup, at right, offers the distinctive fall flavor of sweet winter squash. For the best flavor, be sure you use a sweet onion, such as a Vidalia.

1 Melt the butter in a medium soup pot or a large saucepan. Stir in the onion and rosemary. Partially cover the pan and cook the onion over moderate heat for 10 minutes, stirring occasionally. Stir in the garlic and cook another minute.

2 Add the squash, potatoes, chicken stock, and salt and bring to a boil. Reduce the heat and cover the pot. Cook the soup at a low boil for 20 minutes or until the vegetables are very soft. Remove the pan from the heat.

3 Using a large slotted spoon, transfer the soup solids and a ladleful of broth to a blender or food processor (do this in batches if your appliance is small). Puree the vegetables, then stir them back into the broth. Stir in the pepper, cream, and ham, heating for several minutes before serving. Makes 6 servings.

KIDS' STEPS Kids can measure the ingredients and help add them to the soup pot.

Cheesy Broccoli Soup

INGREDIENTS

- 2 cups peeled, diced all-purpose potatoes
- 2 cups chopped broccoli, plus 1 1/2 cups steamed florets
- 1 cup chopped onion
- 1 carrot, chopped
- 3 garlic cloves
- 1 1/2 teaspoons salt
- 4 cups water
- 1 1/2 cups grated Cheddar cheese
- 3/4 cup milk
- 1/4 teaspoon dill
- 1/4 teaspoon dry mustard
- Black pepper to taste
- 3/4 cup buttermilk

The floating florets of broccoli give this soup its crunch. If your family doesn't finish the whole pot in one sitting, send the leftovers to school in a thermos.

1 In a large soup pot, bring the potatoes, chopped broccoli, onion, carrot, garlic, salt, and water to a boil. Reduce and simmer for 15 minutes.

2 Cool for 10 minutes, then puree the mixture in a blender. Return it to the pot and warm over medium heat, stirring constantly.

3 Add the Cheddar cheese, milk, dill, dry mustard, and pepper, and stir until the cheese melts.

4 Just before serving, add the steamed broccoli florets and buttermilk. Makes 6 to 8 servings.

KIDS' STEPS Kids can measure the ingredients and add them to the soup.

Hearty Beef Stew

INGREDIENTS

1½   pounds stew beef, cut into bite-size pieces (see "What's Your Beef?" on opposite page)

¼   cup plus 3 tablespoons flour

4   tablespoons vegetable oil

1   large onion, coarsely chopped

1   rib celery, thinly sliced

2   to 3 garlic cloves, minced

3   cups beef broth

1   cup tomato juice or vegetable juice

¾   teaspoon salt, plus more to taste

2   bay leaves

2   large all-purpose potatoes, peeled and cut into cubes

2   carrots, peeled and sliced into thin rounds

2   cups fresh green beans, in bite-size pieces

1   teaspoon thyme

1   teaspoon oregano

     Black pepper to taste

1   tablespoon Worcestershire sauce

1   tablespoon light brown sugar

This recipe offers kids lots of fun, hands-on work, but then the waiting game — stewing — begins. The young chefs' patience will be rewarded with the dish's flavorful sauce and tender cubes of beef produced by the slow cooking.

1 Set a soup or stew pot over medium heat for several minutes. Meanwhile, combine the stew beef and ¼ cup of the flour in a gallon-size plastic or paper bag. Shake well to coat the meat.

2 Add 2 tablespoons of the oil to the pot. Swirl the pan to spread the oil around. Add half of the meat to the pan, shaking off any excess flour, and brown it for 3 to 4 minutes, stirring occasionally. Transfer the browned meat to a heatproof dish. Then add the remaining 2 tablespoons of oil to the pan and brown the remaining meat.

3 Stir the onion, celery, garlic, and first batch of meat back into the pan. Sauté the mixture for 3 minutes, stirring often, until the onion wilts.

4 Stir in the broth, tomato juice, ¾ teaspoon salt, and bay leaves. Increase the heat, bringing the liquid to a simmer. Then reduce the heat to low. Cover the pot and gently simmer the stew for 1 hour, stirring several times as it cooks.

5 Stir in the remaining ingredients, except for the reserved 3 tablespoons of flour. Bring the stew to an active simmer, then reduce the heat to low. Cover and simmer gently for 45 minutes more, until the vegetables are tender.

6 To thicken the stew, spoon a ladleful of broth into a small mixing bowl. Whisk in the reserved 3 tablespoons of flour. Then stir the mixture into the stew and simmer for 10 minutes more. Serve with dinner rolls or over rice or egg noodles. Serves 6 to 8.

KIDS' STEPS Kids can coat the meat with flour by shaking it in the plastic bag, sauté it, then sauté the vegetables and add the broth and juice.

TIP: When sautéing the onions, garlic, and celery with the first batch of meat, sauté until the onion wilts.

What's Your Beef?

While the convenience of picking up a package of precut stew meat may be tempting, it can be a pricey option. Plus, you can't be sure what you're getting. For the best-quality stews, buy steaks or roasts and slice them up yourself. Often, particularly if your grocery store is having a sale, you'll pay less per pound for a better cut of beef.

The ones shown below are good choices. Whatever cut you decide to use, keep in mind that stew should never be boiled, lest the meat become tough. Always simmer a stew gently, even when you're reheating it. If your aim is to save time, start with smaller chunks of meat.

CHUCK ROAST

RUMP ROAST

BLADE ROAST

CHAPTER FIVE

BREADS

Start a baking tradition with our no-fail recipes

BREAD IS A TRULY UNIVERSAL FOOD — a staple the world 'round since ancient times. Whether you bake a batch every week or once a year, the simple act of mixing the batter and kneading the dough links you through history and geography to families everywhere. Try a slow-rising variety like our World's Simplest Bread on a relaxed day around the house, or whip up a quick batch of Crispy Corn Bread to serve with soup or stew. Either way, your children will love the thrill of biting into a warm slice of bread they've baked themselves. To help the experience along, try these tips.

STOCK UP ON SUPPLIES. Keep yeast, flour, and other mixings on hand so you're ready to bake whenever the spirit strikes.

STIR UP SOME KITCHEN SCIENCE. More so than cooking, baking is a science — and a natural way to teach kids about measurements, mixing, and basic chemical reactions. Stir yeast and water, add a pinch of sugar, and watch it fizz, or combine the wet and dry ingredients in quick breads and biscuits and look for bubbles. Make our homemade versions of familiar favorites like English muffins, bagels, and popovers, and talk about how the ingredients and cooking methods make each unique.

GET IN SHAPE. Bread doesn't have to be round or square. It can also be braided, rolled, or formed into a heart, a turtle, or a teddy bear. Check out our creative designs, then set your kids loose with a batch of dough.

MAKE IT EASY ON YOURSELF. Mix dry ingredients ahead of time and store them in an airtight container to speed preparation. For fresh biscuits in minutes, stash a batch of our Quick and Easy Biscuit mix in a canister in the fridge, then just add milk, cut, and bake. Whatever bread you're baking, double or triple the recipe and freeze the extra loaves, sealed in plastic bags. (Thaw at room temperature, in the bag, to keep them moist.)

Quick and Easy Biscuits

Play dough is great, but nothing beats the real thing — it's got all that same kneadable, rollable, shapable fun, with the added promise of a fresh-baked treat. Your child will love to help make this wholesome baking mix, and by always keeping some on hand, you can have delicious biscuits in a snap.

BASIC MIX

- 3 cups all-purpose flour
- 1½ cups whole wheat flour
- 1 teaspoon salt
- 2 tablespoons baking powder
- 1 cup cold butter, cut into small pieces

HOMEMADE BISCUITS

- 2 cups mix (above)
- ⅔ cup milk or buttermilk
  Cinnamon sugar (optional)

1 For the mix, whisk the dry ingredients in a large bowl and then use a pastry cutter or fork to blend in the butter until the mixture looks uniformly crumbly. Scoop the mix into a large jar or a gallon-size ziplock bag and store it in the refrigerator for up to 2 weeks.

2 When you're ready to make the biscuits, heat the oven to 425°. Then stir together the 2 cups of mix and the ⅔ cup of milk or buttermilk in a large bowl until a dough forms.

3 Knead the dough a few times, then pat or roll it out, about ½ inch thick, on a lightly floured surface.

4 Use cookie cutters to punch out the biscuits, then place them on a baking sheet. Sprinkle on cinnamon sugar, if you like, then bake until lightly browned, about 10 to 12 minutes. Makes about ten 2-inch biscuits.

 **KIDS' STEPS** Kids can measure and mix the ingredients, roll the dough, and stamp out the biscuits with cookie cutters.

Parmesan Diamond Biscuits

Your kids can lend a hand preparing this biscuit recipe — first by patting and shaping the dough and then by sprinkling and pressing on the Parmesan cheese that gives the biscuits their golden baked finish. The key to making these tasty, light biscuits is handling the dough as little as possible once you've added the buttermilk.

INGREDIENTS

- 2   cups flour
- 1   tablespoon sugar
- 2   teaspoons baking powder
- ½   teaspoon baking soda
- ½   teaspoon salt
- 4   tablespoons cold butter, cut into ¼-inch pieces
- ½   cup freshly grated Parmesan cheese
- ¾   cup plus 2 tablespoons buttermilk

  Extra buttermilk and Parmesan cheese for biscuit topping

1 Heat the oven to 425°. Lightly dust a baking sheet with flour or cornmeal and set it aside. In a large bowl, sift together the flour, sugar, baking powder, baking soda, and salt. Add the butter and cut it into the dry mixture with a pastry cutter until the mixture resembles a coarse meal. Mix in the ½ cup of grated Parmesan.

2 Make a well in the dry ingredients and pour ¾ cup of the buttermilk into it. Stir with a few quick strokes just until a dough forms. Turn the dough onto a floured surface. Knead it gently (4 or 5 times with floured hands), then pat it into a 7-inch square.

KIDS' STEPS Kids can brush the biscuits with the buttermilk and sprinkle on the Parmesan cheese.

3 Slice the dough into diagonal strips and repeat in the other direction to create diamond-shaped biscuits. Use a pastry brush to lightly coat the dough with 2 tablespoons of buttermilk, then sprinkle on the Parmesan, gently pressing it into the surface.

4 Transfer the biscuits to the baking sheet, leaving some room between them. Set the baking sheet on the center oven rack and bake until golden brown, about 15 minutes. Place the biscuits in a cloth-lined basket and serve warm. Makes 15 to 18 small biscuits.

Perfect Popovers

With its crusty outside and slightly moist inside, a popover spread with butter and jam is hard to resist. Plus, this recipe gives young chefs an exciting introduction to the science of cooking. As the batter bakes in a hot oven, it fills with steam, rising high in the pan and popping over the sides.

INGREDIENTS

- 2 large eggs
- 1 cup milk
- 1 cup flour
   Scant ½ teaspoon salt
- 2 tablespoons melted butter

1 Lightly grease a 6-cup popover pan (or 6 large muffin-pan cups). Be sure to also grease the top of the pan (or the rims of the muffin cups).

2 Whisk the eggs in a medium bowl until frothy. Whisk in the milk. Sift the flour and salt into the bowl and whisk for 30 seconds, until smooth and lump-free. Then whisk in the melted butter. Set the batter aside for 15 minutes.
TIP: You can mix up all the ingredients in a blender for lump-free batter.

3 While you're waiting, adjust the oven rack to the center position and heat the oven to 425°.

4 When you're ready to bake, whisk the batter again until smooth, then pour it into a 2-cup glass measuring cup or pitcher. Then pour the batter into the cups, dividing it evenly (the cups should be about two thirds full).

5 Bake the popovers for 25 minutes, then reduce the heat to 375° (350° if you're using a dark pan) and bake for an additional 10 minutes; do not open the oven to check on them before the 35 minutes have elapsed. When done, the popovers will be tall, domed, and have a rich golden-brown color.

6 Remove the pan from the oven and use a sharp knife to poke a small hole in the top of each popover so the steam can escape. Allow them to cool in the pan for a minute or two, then remove them — they should pop right out. Wait another minute or so, then carefully tear open the popovers, being sure to avoid any remaining steam. Eat them plain or spread with butter and jam or apple butter. Makes 6 popovers.

KIDS' STEPS Younger kids can measure and mix the ingredients. Older kids can pour the batter into the baking cups and carefully pierce the popovers to release the steam when they are done.

FUN FACT
Why Does a Popover Rise?

Many baked goods require baking powder, baking soda, or yeast to rise as they cook, but popovers are different. Popover batter has enough liquid in it to create steam, which gets trapped inside the popover's shell. As the steam builds, the shell inflates like a bubble-gum bubble until it becomes too hard and crispy to expand any more. The steam remains inside a popover for a while after it is finished baking, so be very careful when you first tear it open.

Banana Bread

INGREDIENTS

- 2   cups flour
- 1   teaspoon baking powder
- 1/2   teaspoon baking soda
- 1/2   teaspoon salt
- 1/2   cup (1 stick) butter, softened
- 1   cup sugar
- 2   eggs, room temperature
- 1   teaspoon vanilla extract
- 3   medium-large very ripe bananas
- 1/2   cup sour cream
- 1/3   cup chopped walnuts (optional)

Those neglected bananas lying on your kitchen counter may be too brown for lunch, but they're perfect for baking. Soft and sweet, they make banana bread moist and delicious. Toss in some chopped walnuts — or dried cranberries or mini chocolate chips — and you've got a wholesome bread that's just right for a lunch box or after-school snack.

1 Heat the oven to 325°. Line a 5- by 9-inch loaf pan, preferably one with a light interior, with enough waxed paper to drape over the ends and sides. This will make the baked bread a cinch to remove and the pan easy to clean.

2 Sift the flour, baking powder, baking soda, and salt into a medium bowl. In a large bowl, cream the butter using an electric mixer. Gradually add the sugar, scraping down the sides of the bowl as necessary. Add the eggs one at a time, beating well after each addition. Add the vanilla extract and blend briefly.

3 Peel the bananas and place them in a separate bowl. Mash them with a fork or a potato masher. Add the sour cream and stir to blend.

4 Using a wooden spoon, blend a third of the dry mixture into the butter-sugar mixture. Stirring just enough to blend (overmixing will make the bread turn out chewy), add the rest of the ingredients in the following order: half of the banana mixture, half of the remaining dry mixture, the rest of the banana mixture, the rest of the dry mixture. Stir in the walnuts, or the ingredients for the bread variations listed below.

5 Scrape the batter into the prepared pan and smooth the top with a spoon. Bake on the center oven rack until a tester inserted deep into the center of the bread comes out clean, about 70 to 75 minutes.

6 Transfer the bread to a wire cooling rack and cool it in the pan for about 20 minutes. Using the waxed paper, lift the bread from the pan and place it on the rack. Pull down the sides of the paper and allow the bread to cool thoroughly before slicing. Makes 10 or more servings.

CRANBERRY BANANA BREAD: Stir 1 cup dried cranberries into the batter at the end of step 4.

CHOCOLATE CHIP WALNUT BANANA BREAD: Stir 2/3 cup mini chocolate chips and 1/3 cup chopped walnuts into the batter at the end of step 4.

KIDS' STEPS   Older kids can crack the eggs and flip the omelet. Younger kids can beat the eggs.

Cranberry Soda Bread

If you're not already a fan of soda breads, you will be after you've tried this variation that includes cranberries. To achieve the right texture, cool the bread before serving.

INGREDIENTS

Oil, for pan

Cornmeal, for dusting pan

1/2 cup old-fashioned oats

1 3/4 cups buttermilk

1/3 cup honey

2 tablespoons vegetable oil

3 cups all-purpose flour

1/2 cup whole wheat flour

1 1/2 teaspoons salt

1 teaspoon baking soda

1 teaspoon baking powder

1 cup dried sweetened cranberries

1 Heat the oven to 400°. Lightly oil a large baking sheet and dust it with cornmeal. Measure the oats into a bowl, then stir in the buttermilk, honey, and oil.

2 In a large bowl, combine the remaining ingredients and make a well in the middle. Pour the liquid into it and stir briskly with a wooden spoon until the dough pulls together in a shaggy mass.

3 Let the dough rest for 3 minutes, then turn it onto a floured surface and gently knead it for about 30 seconds.

KIDS' STEPS Kids can measure and mix the ingredients and shape the dough into loaves.

4 Divide the dough in half and form each half into a football shape with rounded ends. Place the loaves on the baking sheet with plenty of room between them and cut a shallow slit down the center of each.

5 Bake the bread for 20 minutes, then reduce the heat to 375° and bake 25 minutes more or until the loaves are golden and crusty and the bottoms sound hollow when tapped. Makes 2 loaves.

Zucchini Bread

Cheerfully flecked with green, this classic zucchini loaf bakes up high and is not too sweet. And, it's a great way to get kids to eat their vegetables.

INGREDIENTS

- 3 eggs
- 1 cup vegetable oil
- 1 cup sugar
- 2 cups grated unpeeled zucchini
- 1 cup chopped walnuts (optional)
- 2 cups flour
- 1 teaspoon baking soda
- 1 tablespoon baking powder
- 1 teaspoon salt
- 1 teaspoon cinnamon
- $1/2$ teaspoon nutmeg

1 Heat the oven to 350° and grease a 9- by 5-inch loaf pan. Combine the eggs, oil, and sugar in a large bowl and mix until well combined. Stir in the zucchini and, if desired, the walnuts.

2 In a separate bowl, combine the flour, baking soda, baking powder, salt, cinnamon, and nutmeg and stir well. Pour the dry ingredients over the zucchini mixture and stir until well combined.

3 Pour the mixture into the loaf pan and bake until a toothpick inserted in the middle comes out clean, about 65 to 70 minutes. Makes 1 loaf.

KIDS' STEPS Older kids can grate the zucchini (have them do it over waxed paper for easy cleanup). Younger kids can measure and mix the ingredients.

Crispy Corn Bread

When baked and served in a big cast-iron skillet, this corn bread has a rustic, straight-from-the-campfire look — the edges and surface come out crispy and beautifully browned.

INGREDIENTS

- 3   tablespoons butter
- 1   cup flour
- 1   cup fine yellow cornmeal
- 2   tablespoons sugar
- 1   teaspoon baking soda
- 1   teaspoon baking powder
- 1/2   teaspoon salt
- 2   large eggs, lightly beaten
- 2   cups buttermilk

1 Heat the oven to 400°. Put the butter in a 10-inch cast-iron skillet (or a 10-inch deep-dish pie pan) and place it in the oven while you prepare the batter.

2 Sift the flour, cornmeal, sugar, baking soda, baking powder, and salt into a large bowl. In a separate bowl, blend the eggs and buttermilk.

3 When the butter has melted, remove the skillet from the oven.

Swirl the pan to spread the butter, then pour most of the butter into the liquid ingredients. Make a well in the dry ingredients and add the liquid. Stir the batter until evenly mixed, then carefully pour it into the hot skillet.

4 Bake the bread for 25 to 30 minutes or until the top is golden and crusty, then cool it in the pan on a wire rack for 10 minutes before slicing. Makes 10 servings.

KIDS' STEPS Kids can sift the dry ingredients into the bowl and blend the eggs and buttermilk together.

Pumpkin Bread

Any way you slice it, this pumpkin spice bread won't last long once your kids take a bite. That's why this recipe makes two loaves.

INGREDIENTS

- 2   cups canned pumpkin
- 3   cups sugar
- 1   cup water
- 1   cup vegetable oil
- 4   eggs
- 3 1/3   cups flour
- 2   teaspoons baking soda
- 2   teaspoons cinnamon
- 1   teaspoon salt
- 1   teaspoon baking powder
- 1/2   teaspoon nutmeg
- 3/4   teaspoon ground cloves

1 Heat the oven to 350°. In a large mixing bowl, combine the pumpkin, sugar, water, oil, and eggs. Beat until well mixed.

2 In a separate bowl, combine the flour, baking soda, cinnamon, salt, baking powder, nutmeg, and cloves and stir until combined. Slowly add the dry ingredients to the pumpkin mixture, beating until smooth.

3 Grease two 9- by 5-inch loaf pans and dust them with flour. Evenly divide the batter between them. Bake until a toothpick inserted into the center comes out clean, about 60 to 70 minutes. Cool for 10 to 15 minutes.

4 Remove the bread from the pans by inverting them onto a rack and tapping the bottoms. Slice and serve plain, buttered, or with cream cheese.

KIDS' STEPS Kids can measure and mix the ingredients.

World's Simplest Bread

This unfussy recipe won't dirty every bowl in the kitchen, collapse during the inevitable interruptions, or yield to your child's desire to treat it like a mound of clay. You can use this master recipe, inspired by the King Arthur Flour bread recipe, to shape two traditional loaves or the turtle bread below.

INGREDIENTS

2 cups warm (110° F) water (for a tender, brown crust use 1/2 cup warm water and 1 1/2 cups warm milk)

1 tablespoon active dry yeast

1 tablespoon sugar

5 1/2 to 6 cups all-purpose flour (for whole wheat bread, use whole wheat flour)

2 teaspoons salt

1 Pour the warm water into a large bowl. The key to activating yeast is finding the right water temperature. Don't let this intimidate you; just think bathwater. If it feels warm on the wrist, but not hot, it's ready to pour into a bowl.

2 Add the yeast and sugar and whisk until they are dissolved.

3 Measure 2 cups of the flour into the bowl and whisk the mixture well. Let the batter "proof," or sit, for 10 minutes. If tiny bubbles appear and the batter looks slightly expanded, you're on the right track.

4 Stir in the salt, then add the remaining flour, 1 cup at a time.

5 Turn the dough onto a lightly floured surface and knead it until it is smooth and elastic, about 10 minutes.

TIP: To get the hang of kneading, think of it as a three-step process: push, turn, fold. First, push down on the dough; next, give it a quarter-turn clockwise; then fold the dough over on itself and start again, as shown in the first 3 steps at right.

6 Place the ball in a bowl greased with vegetable oil and turn to coat. Cover with a damp cloth or plastic wrap and let the dough rise in a draft-free area for 1 to 2 hours, or until it has doubled in size.

7 Punch the dough down, then knead it again to remove air bubbles. Divide the dough in half and roll each portion of it into a rectangle. Fold each rectangle into thirds like a letter. Turn the ends under and place each portion, seam side down, into a greased 9- by 5-inch loaf pan. Cover with plastic wrap or a damp cloth and let rise again for about 45 minutes.

8 Heat the oven to 400° and bake the bread for 30 minutes. Remove the bread from the oven; if the bottom of the loaf sounds hollow when tapped, it's done.

9 Cool in the pan for 10 minutes, then transfer to a wire rack. Rub with butter for a shiny finish. Makes 2 loaves.

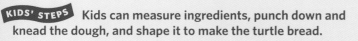 **KIDS' STEPS** Kids can measure ingredients, punch down and knead the dough, and shape it to make the turtle bread.

FUN FOOD

Shaping Turtle Bread

After the bread dough has risen once, punch it down and form balls for the shell (about 6 inches in diameter), the head (3 inches), and the legs (2 inches) and assemble on a greased baking sheet (as seen at right), adding a dough tail.

Texturize the shell's top by etching a crisscross pattern with a knife. Push two raisins in the head for eyes. Cover the dough with plastic and let it rise again for 30 minutes. Heat the oven to 375°. Meanwhile, make an egg wash by whisking an egg with 1 tablespoon of water. Brush the dough lightly with the egg wash and bake until golden brown, about 25 minutes. For more reptilian realism, add a couple of drops of green food coloring to the egg wash.

Challah Bread

Breaking bread together is particularly rewarding with this recipe from Roberta DesBouillons, founder of the children's cooking school Apron Strings.

INGREDIENTS

½	cup plus ⅔ cup warm water (110° F)
2	teaspoons active dry yeast
¾	cup plus 1 tablespoon sugar
5	eggs
1	cup vegetable oil
2	teaspoons salt
7	cups flour
1	large egg yolk
1	tablespoon water

1 Combine ½ cup of the warm water, the yeast, and 1 tablespoon of sugar in a small bowl and stir to dissolve the yeast. Let it "proof," or sit, in a warm spot until foamy, about 10 minutes.

2 Beat the eggs until foamy. Add the dissolved yeast, oil, salt, and remaining ¾ cup of sugar and beat until the mixture is pale yellow and slightly thickened, about 4 minutes. Add ⅔ cup of warm water and beat to blend.

3 Stir in ½ cup of flour at a time until the dough no longer sticks to the bowl. Knead the dough on a lightly floured surface until smooth and elastic, adding a little flour if it's too sticky.

4 Put the dough in a lightly oiled large bowl, turning it once to coat. Cover the bowl with plastic wrap and top with a kitchen towel. Let the dough rise in a warm, draft-free spot until doubled, about 1 hour. Punch down the dough, cover the bowl as before, and let the dough rise 30 minutes more.

5 Grease 2 medium baking sheets. Turn the dough onto a lightly floured surface and divide it in half. Divide each half into 3 equal pieces and roll them into 9-inch ropes. For each loaf, braid together 3 ropes, working on a prepared baking sheet. Cover each loaf with a towel and let the dough rise until almost doubled, about 30 minutes. Meanwhile, heat the oven to 400°.

6 Whisk together the egg yolk and 1 tablespoon of water and lightly brush the mixture on the loaf tops. Bake the bread for 10 minutes, then lower the oven to 350° and bake until the loaves are golden brown and sound hollow when tapped on the bottom, about 35 minutes. Makes 2 loaves.

KIDS' STEPS Kids can measure and mix the ingredients and help braid the dough.

PREP TIME: **20 minutes** RISING TIME: **1 hour** BAKING TIME: **about 50 minutes**

Anadama Bread

Legend says this flavorful batter bread was created by a frustrated farmer whose wife, Ana, never baked. Because it needs to rise only once, it's a great recipe for kids to help with.

INGREDIENTS

- 2 cups boiling water
- 2 tablespoons butter
- 1/2 cup yellow cornmeal
- 1 package (1/4 ounce) active dry yeast
- 1/2 cup warm water (110° F)
- 3/4 cup molasses
- 1 1/2 teaspoons salt
- 4 2/3 cups flour

1 Carefully pour the boiling water into a large bowl. Add the butter and sprinkle in the cornmeal, whisking to mix. Let the mixture stand until lukewarm.

2 In a small bowl, dissolve the yeast in the warm water. Stir the dissolved yeast, molasses, and salt into the cornmeal, then beat in the flour.

3 Spoon the batter into two buttered 9- by 5-inch loaf pans, cover, and let rise until doubled in bulk (about 1 hour).

4 Heat the oven to 350°. Bake the bread for 45 to 50 minutes until done. Turn the loaves onto wire racks to cool. Makes 2 loaves.

KIDS' STEPS Kids can dissolve the yeast in the warm water and help mix in the ingredients to make the batter.

COOKING BASICS
Proofing 101

Dry yeast granules become active — producing the gases that make dough rise — when you put them in warm water. The way to tell if the yeast is active is by proofing it. To proof, sprinkle a pinch of sugar into the dissolved yeast and wait a few minutes to see if the mixture foams slightly. If it does, the yeast is still good and will do its job of making the dough rise.

English Muffins

This recipe calls for the dough to rise just once, which means you can make and eat the muffins on the same (leisurely) morning. Have the kids split them open with a fork, not a knife, to create those famous nooks and crannies.

INGREDIENTS

- 1 cup milk
- 3 tablespoons butter, cut into pieces
- 2 tablespoons honey
- 1 cup warm water (110° F)
- 1 package (¼ ounce) active dry yeast
- Cornmeal
- 5 ½ to 6 cups flour
- 1 teaspoon salt

TIP: To make heart-shaped English muffins, use a knife or scissors to cut a third of the way into the circle, round the cut side into the top of the heart, and then pinch the opposite side into a point for the tip.

1 Combine the milk, butter, and honey in a medium saucepan. Warm the mixture over medium-low heat until the butter starts to melt, then whisk it briefly. Remove the pan from the heat and allow the liquid to cool until lukewarm.

2 While the milk cools, pour the water into a medium mixing bowl and sprinkle the yeast over it. Stir the liquid gently with a fork and set it aside for 5 to 10 minutes, until all of the yeast has dissolved.

3 Line two baking sheets with waxed paper and sprinkle on a generous amount of cornmeal. (This is where you'll set the muffins to rise.)

4 Pour the cooled milk into the dissolved yeast and gently stir the mixture until well blended. Add 3 cups of flour and the salt to the liquid and beat the mixture vigorously with a wooden spoon until smooth (about 100 strokes). Beat in enough of the remaining flour, about ⅓ cup at a time, so that the dough is firm enough to knead and no longer sticky.

5 Scrape the dough from the bowl onto a floured surface. Dust the top of the dough with flour. Flour your hands, then knead the dough for 3 to 4 minutes. Let the dough rest for about 5 minutes.

6 Roll out the dough with a rolling pin, starting in the middle and pushing the

pin from the center out, until the dough is a half inch thick.

7 Cut the dough into circles with a 3½-inch biscuit cutter. Gather and reroll the scraps and cut out more circles (you should end up with 18). Now shape each circle into a heart as described in the tip at left.

8 Transfer the muffins to the prepared baking sheets, spacing them well apart. Sprinkle cornmeal on the tops. Cover the muffins with a dry, lightweight towel and let them rise until they are almost doubled in height — about 35 to 45 minutes.

9 When the muffins have risen, heat a large, heavy, ungreased skillet over medium heat. (If you have two skillets, you may want to prepare both so you can cook more muffins at once.) Or you can use an electric griddle heated to 300°. Carefully lift the muffins from the waxed paper and place them in the heated pan or griddle, spacing them an inch or so apart. You should be able to fit 4 or 5 muffins in each pan.

10 Cook the muffins for about 10 minutes on each side, using a spatula to flip them. You may have to adjust the heat if the muffins are browning too quickly or slowly. Transfer each batch of cooked muffins to a wire rack to cool before splitting and toasting them. Makes 1½ dozen.

 KIDS' STEPS Kids can knead the dough and shape it into hearts.

Homemade Pretzels

Invite your kids to help you cook up a snack with a real twist. Topped with salt or cinnamon sugar, this home-baked treat can be personalized to suit individual tastes.

INGREDIENTS

1 ½   cups warm water (110°F)

1   tablespoon sugar

1   package (¼ ounce) active dry yeast

4   to 4 ½ cups flour

1   tablespoon salt

    Vegetable oil (for greasing bowl)

2   tablespoons baking soda

1   egg, beaten

1   to 2 tablespoons melted butter

    Coarse salt or cinnamon sugar (for toppings)

1 Measure the water into a mixing bowl. Sprinkle in the sugar and yeast and stir gently to dissolve. Then stir in 3 cups of the flour and the salt until combined. Gather the dough in your hands and place it on a floured surface. Knead the dough, working in more flour a little at a time until you have a soft dough that doesn't stick. Continue kneading for an additional 8 minutes.

2 Place the dough in a large bowl that's been greased with vegetable oil. Turn the dough over a couple of times until it is lightly coated with oil. Then cover the bowl with plastic wrap and place it in a warm spot until the dough rises to double its size, about an hour.

3 Heat the oven to 450°. Punch down the dough and divide it into 16 pieces. Show your child how to roll each piece into an 18-inch strip and then twist it into a pretzel shape.

4 Fill a large stainless steel pot (not aluminum) with 3 inches of water. Bring the water to a boil, then reduce the heat and keep the water at a simmer. Add the baking soda to the water. Now gently drop the pretzels into the simmering water (a parent's job) and poach them for 1 minute. Use a slotted spoon to transfer the pretzels to a greased cookie sheet. Brush on beaten egg, and if you prefer salted pretzels, salt them now.

5 Bake the pretzels for 10 to 12 minutes, until golden. Brush on melted butter, and if you're making sweet pretzels, roll them in cinnamon sugar. Makes 16 pretzels.

KIDS' STEPS   Kids can punch down the dough, divide it into strips, and twist it into pretzel shapes.

Fresh-Baked Bagels

There's no mistaking the difference between packaged, store-bought bagels and ones that are fresh-baked. So although it takes a little time, making a batch from scratch can be quite rewarding — and fun. After shaping the dough into balls and poking holes in the centers, your kids will get a kick out of watching their homemade bagels quickly boil and then bake to perfection.

INGREDIENTS

1½ cups warm water (110° F)
1 package (¼ ounce) active dry yeast (not quick-rising)
4 tablespoons sugar
2½ teaspoons salt
3½ to 3¾ cups flour
1 egg white
1½ teaspoons water
Sesame or poppy seeds (optional)

1 Pour ¼ cup of the water into a small bowl and sprinkle the yeast over it. Stir with a fork, then let the mixture sit for 5 minutes so that the yeast can thoroughly dissolve.

2 Combine the remaining 1¼ cups of water and the dissolved yeast in a large mixing bowl. Stir in 3 tablespoons of the sugar, then stir in the salt. Add 2 cups of the flour and stir by hand to blend well.

3 Stir in enough of the remaining flour, about ¼ cup at a time, to make a dough that's firm enough to knead. Turn the dough out onto a floured surface and knead it with floured hands for about 10 minutes, using as much of the remaining flour as necessary to keep the dough from sticking. When fully kneaded, the dough will be firm but supple and should hold the imprint of your hand.

4 Transfer the dough to an oiled bowl, turning it a few times to coat the entire surface. Cover with plastic wrap and place it in a warm, draft-free spot until it has doubled in bulk, about 1 hour.

5 When the dough is ready, punch it down. Turn it out onto a floured surface and knead it for 1 minute. Divide the dough in half, then divide each half into 4 equal pieces. Shape the 8 pieces into balls, placing them on a floured work counter and dusting the tops with flour. Let them rest for 2 to 3 minutes, then flatten them slightly with your fingers.

6 Fill a large soup pot about two thirds with water. Add the remaining 1 tablespoon of sugar and bring to a boil.

7 Working with 1 ball of dough at a time, press your floured thumb down through the center to make a hole. Stretch the dough slightly so the hole is about 1 inch in diameter. It will look like a doughnut. Set the bagels aside on a floured surface, covering them loosely with plastic wrap or waxed paper.

8 Let the bagels rest for 10 minutes Meanwhile, grease a large baking sheet and set it aside. Heat the oven to 400°.

9 Gently drop two of the bagels into the boiling water (a parent's job). They should float, but don't worry if they sink initially — they'll quickly rise to the surface. Boil them for 30 seconds on one side, then carefully turn them with a long-handled, slotted spoon and boil them for another 30 seconds.

10 Using your slotted spoon, transfer the bagels to a clean tea towel to drain. Wait a few seconds, then transfer them to the baking sheet, leaving space between them. Repeat with the remaining bagels.

11 Make a glaze for the bagel tops by whisking the egg white and water in a small bowl until frothy. Using a pastry brush, coat the surface of the bagels with the glaze. Sprinkle on sesame seeds or poppy seeds, if desired.

12 Bake the bagels on the center oven rack until they are deep golden brown, about 25 minutes. Then transfer them to a wire rack to cool. Makes 8 bagels.

KIDS' STEPS Older kids can roll the dough into balls and shape them into bagels. Younger kids can brush on the glaze and sprinkle on the seeds.

Sweet Cinnamon Rolls

DOUGH

¼ cup warm water (110° F)

1 package (¼ ounce) active dry yeast

1 cup warm milk

⅓ cup sugar

1 large egg, lightly beaten

2 teaspoons vanilla extract

3 ¾ to 4 cups flour

1 ½ teaspoons salt

4 tablespoons butter, softened

FILLING

¾ cup packed light brown sugar

¾ cup walnuts or pecans, chopped

2 teaspoons cinnamon

4 tablespoons butter, softened

SWEET GLAZE TOPPING

1 ½ cups confectioners' sugar

2 ½ tablespoons milk or light cream

2 tablespoons melted butter

1 to 2 drops vanilla extract

You don't have to go to your local bakery to find great-tasting cinnamon rolls made from scratch. With this recipe, your child can bake a sweet and buttery batch everyone in the family will find irresistible.

1 Pour the water into a small bowl. Sprinkle in the yeast and let it dissolve (about 5 minutes). In a large bowl, stir together the warm milk and sugar. Then stir in the dissolved yeast, egg, and vanilla extract.

2 With a wooden spoon, stir 2 cups of the flour into the liquid, then beat well. Cover the bowl with plastic wrap and leave the sponge (see sidebar on opposite page) undisturbed for 15 minutes.

3 Stir the salt and then the soft butter into the sponge. Add the remaining flour, about ⅓ cup at a time, stirring well each time. When the dough balls up and becomes impossible to stir, flour your hands and knead the dough right in the bowl for 2 to 3 minutes.

4 Transfer the dough to a well-floured counter and continue to knead it for about 6 to 7 more minutes, until it's smooth and elastic. Put the dough in a large, clean, lightly oiled bowl, turning to coat the entire surface. Cover the bowl with plastic wrap and set it aside in a

warm, draft-free spot until the dough doubles (about 1 hour). Meanwhile, prepare the filling. Stir together the brown sugar, nuts, and cinnamon in a small bowl until well combined.

5 When the dough has risen, punch it down several times to deflate it. Then knead the dough again on a lightly floured surface for 1 minute. Cover the dough with plastic wrap and let it rest for 10 to 15 minutes. Butter a 13- by 9-inch baking pan.

6 Reflour your working area and, using a floured rolling pin, roll the dough into a 12- by 16-inch rectangle so that a long edge is closest to you. If the dough springs back (it should stay where you've rolled it), let it rest another 2 or 3 minutes.

7 Spread the softened butter over the dough, leaving a 1-inch border along each of the long edges. Cover the butter evenly with the cinnamon-nut mixture, pressing it down gently. Lightly moisten both long edges with water.

KIDS' STEPS Older kids can sprinkle the cinnamon mixture on the dough and roll it up. Younger kids can drizzle on the glaze.

TIP: Starting at the long edge closest to you, snugly roll up the dough like a rug.

8 Starting at the long edge closest to you, snugly roll up the dough like a rug. Pinch the seam together. With a sharp serrated knife, score the dough in the center, then at the center of each half. With those marks as guides, cut the dough into 12 equal pieces.

9 Evenly space the rolls in the pan, brushing the outer edges with a little melted butter (to keep them from sticking together as they bake). Cover the pan with plastic wrap and let the rolls rise until nearly doubled, about 35 to 45 minutes. Heat the oven to 350° near the end of the rising.

10 Remove the plastic and bake the rolls on the center rack for about 30 minutes, until golden and cooked through. Run a spatula around the pan to loosen the rolls, then invert them onto a large baking sheet. Carefully pull apart the rolls and set them right side up on a cooling rack for 15 to 20 minutes.

11 While the rolls cool, you can whisk up the Sweet Glaze for the top. Combine all the glaze ingredients and whisk to blend. The glaze should be smooth and flowing, but not overly runny. Add a little extra milk or cream, if need be, to reach desired consistency. Drizzle on the rolls. Serve warm. Makes 12 large rolls.

COOKING BASICS
Sponge
• • • • • • • • • • • • • • • • • • • •

No, we're not referring to a popular square TV star here, but rather to the dough mixture in the early stage of bread making. While the dough is covered and resting, bubbles form and make a light, spongy batter. Then other ingredients are added.

CHAPTER SIX

DINNER

Please everyone at the table with these quick and easy family favorites

COMING UP, NIGHT AFTER NIGHT, with healthy, easy-to-make suppers that satisfy everyone at the table is one of parenting's greatest challenges. In this chapter, you'll find our favorites from years on the front lines of family dinners. Your kids can help you cook up nutritious versions of fast foods, such as Simple Sam-Burgers and Potato Chip Chicken Fingers. Or try our kid- and parent-pleasing variations of international fare like Mexicali Pie. And for the purists in your family, there are classics such as Kids' First Mac and Cheese. The recipes that follow, along with the tips below, can make memorable family dinners easy.

PLAN AHEAD. With your kids' help, create a roster of quickie suppers that use foods you always have on hand. Post it — along with a list of the necessary ingredients — inside a cupboard door, for easy reference on nights when time is tight.

CUSTOMIZE IT. Serve toppings and fillings separately, and let picky kids — and adults — assemble personalized variations of the meal. Instead of tossing together all the ingredients for a pasta dish, for example, set out separate bowls of cooked veggies, meat, and sauce, so family members can toss their own. And don't forget to adapt our recipes, adding and omitting ingredients as needed, to fit your family's tastes.

SHARE THE JOB. *FamilyFun* reader Heather Sciford of Omaha, Nebraska, lets each family member choose the menu for one dinner a week. Fellow reader Dorris Creter of Sarasota, Florida, created a weekly Kids Cook Night, on which her two children choose the meal, shop for ingredients, and make or buy dessert.

VARY THE ROUTINE. Once a week, *FamilyFun* reader Rebecca Bean of Martinez, Georgia, serves breakfast for dinner. The Wingfields of Paso Robles, California, make learning fun and tasty. Their History Nights pair period recipes with educational DVDs. However you choose to mix things up, you'll find variety is the spice of supper.

Simple Sam-Burgers

Grillmaster and *FamilyFun* senior editor Sam Mead says these spiffed-up burgers are such a hit with his young daughter, Ruby, she goes right for the burger and forgets about the bun.

MY GREAT IDEA

Hearty Hamburgers

• • • • • • • • • • • • • • • • • • •

Love is rare — or better yet, in the case of the Aydinel family's valentine hamburgers, medium-well. A heart-shaped cookie cutter used on both the raw meat and the bun is all you need (for sanitation's sake, use it on the bun first). Suzy and Michael Aydinel's older kids — Christine, 6, and Michael, 4 (Suzy, 11 months, just watches) — like to draw ketchup faces on their burgers before digging in.

INGREDIENTS

- 1   to 1 1/4 pounds ground beef
- 3   tablespoons steak sauce (such as A.1.)
- 1   tablespoon Dijon mustard
- 1/2   teaspoon salt
- 1/4   teaspoon pepper
- 2   cloves garlic, minced
- 2   teaspoons minced fresh oregano, or 3/4 teaspoon dried
- 1   to 2 tablespoons finely minced onion

  Cheese (optional)

1 Combine all of the ingredients in a large mixing bowl, mixing thoroughly with your hands or a wooden spoon. Shape into 4 patties by hand, making the center of each just a little thinner than the edges. Refrigerate until ready to grill.

2 Start your grill, and when it's good and hot, grill the burgers to the desired doneness, flipping once. They'll take about 4 minutes on each side, more or less, depending on how you like them cooked. To make cheeseburgers, top with slices of American cheese or sharp Cheddar cheese after you flip them. Makes 4 burgers.

KIDS' STEPS Kids can measure the ingredients and help shape the patties, washing their hands after handling the raw meat.

Philly Cheesesteak Sandwich

Hearty enough to be served for dinner, this sandwich is pretty true to the Philadelphia original, but we've made a few modifications, including adding peppers and using Provolone cheese rather than the more traditional Cheez Whiz.

INGREDIENTS

1½	pounds boneless rib eye or top round steak
3	tablespoons vegetable oil
1	very large onion, halved and thinly sliced
1	large green bell pepper, cut in strips
1	large red bell pepper, cut in strips
1	clove garlic, minced
½	teaspoon salt
⅛	teaspoon pepper
¼	teaspoon Tabasco sauce
4	soft Italian or hoagie rolls (6-inch)
½	pound Provolone cheese, grated

1 To make the steak easier to slice, set it in the freezer for about 45 minutes to 1 hour. Remove the steak from the freezer and cut it into very thin slices, ⅛ inch or thinner, and set it aside. Heat the oven to 400°.

2 Heat 2 tablespoons of the oil in a large skillet. Add the onion and peppers and sauté over medium heat for about 8 to 10 minutes, stirring occasionally, until softened. Stir in the garlic, ¼ teaspoon of the salt, and the pepper and cook over high heat for another minute. Transfer the mixture to a bowl and set it aside.

3 Add the remaining 1 tablespoon of oil to the skillet. Stir in the meat and cook over high heat for 4 minutes, or until done, then add the other ¼ teaspoon of salt. Add the Tabasco and stir. Return the vegetables to the skillet, stir, and heat the mixture through. Cover the skillet and turn off the heat.

4 Slice the rolls lengthwise and arrange on a large baking sheet. Pile the filling onto the bottom half of each roll and sprinkle generously with the cheese. Heat the sandwiches in the oven for about 5 minutes, until the cheese melts. For smaller appetites, slice the sandwiches in half before serving. Serves 4 to 6.

KIDS' STEPS Older kids can cut and sauté the vegetables. Younger kids can sprinkle the cheese on the sandwiches.

Beef and Broccoli Lo Mein

When you're in the mood for lo mein, you can always get takeout, but here's an easy recipe that actually takes less time to prepare than you'd spend waiting for your order. For the beef, sirloin tips are ideal, but you can also make this dish with flank steak.

INGREDIENTS

- 8 ounces thin spaghetti, broken in half
- 1 teaspoon dark sesame oil
- 1 tablespoon vegetable oil
- 3 cups chopped broccoli
- 1 ½ cups thinly sliced onion
- 1 tablespoon peeled, grated fresh ginger
- 4 garlic cloves, minced
- 12 ounces sirloin tips, cut crosswise into thin strips
- 3 tablespoons beef broth
- 3 tablespoons soy sauce
- 2 tablespoons brown sugar
- 1 tablespoon oyster-flavored sauce

1 Stir the spaghetti into a pot of lightly salted boiling water and cook it until it is done. (While the pasta is cooking, prepare your vegetables.) Drain the noodles well, then return them to the pot and toss them with the sesame oil.

2 Heat the vegetable oil in a large skillet over medium-high heat. Add the broccoli and onion and cook for 3 minutes, stirring often. Add the ginger and garlic and continue stirring while the mixture cooks for another 30 seconds. Add the sirloin and cook it, stirring often, for 5 minutes or until it is no longer pink.

3 In a small bowl, mix the broth, soy sauce, brown sugar, and oyster sauce. Add this mixture and the pasta to the skillet and continue cooking, stirring often, until everything is heated through. Serve hot. Makes 4 to 6 servings.

KIDS' STEPS Older kids can grate the ginger. Younger kids can measure and mix the sauce.

PREP TIME: **20 minutes**   MARINATING TIME: **30 minutes**   COOKING TIME: **about 10 minutes**

Steak Stir-Fry

This easy-to-make stir-fry, with tender beef and a sesame sauce, is topped with pea pods, but broccoli also blends nicely with the sweet flavors.

INGREDIENTS

2	tablespoons soy sauce
1	tablespoon rice wine vinegar
1	tablespoon sugar
1/2	teaspoon sesame oil
2 1/2	teaspoons cornstarch
1	garlic clove, minced
1	teaspoon peeled, grated fresh ginger
3/4	pound flank steak
2	tablespoons vegetable oil
8	ounces pea pods, trimmed
1	medium red bell pepper, cut into 1/4-inch-wide strips
1/2	cup chicken broth
2	tablespoons oyster-flavored sauce

1 Make the marinade for the meat by measuring the soy sauce, rice wine vinegar, sugar, and sesame oil into a medium bowl. Add the cornstarch and blend it in with the back of a spoon. Stir in the garlic and ginger.

KIDS' STEPS Kids can measure and stir the ingredients for the marinade.

2 Trim any fat from the steak. Cut into pieces about 1½ inches long and not quite ¼ inch thick. Stir the meat into the marinade. Cover and set it aside for 30 minutes to marinate.

3 Heat a wok or large sauté pan. If you're using a wok, drizzle the 2 tablespoons of oil around the inside near the top (it will run down and coat the sides sufficiently). Otherwise, gently rotate the pan to evenly spread the oil. Add the meat, spreading it out in the pan, and stir-fry it for 2 to 3 minutes or until it is well browned.

4 Use a slotted spoon to transfer the cooked meat to a plate. Immediately add the pea pods, pepper, and chicken broth to the pan. Cook, uncovered, over high heat 1 to 3 minutes stirring occasionally. Stir in the meat and oyster sauce. Cook for another minute or two, until the vegetables are tender. Makes 4 servings.

LEARNING TIP
Using Chopsticks

Chinese food just seems to taste better when you eat it with chopsticks. Using them is also a great way to slow the meal to an enjoyable pace. Granted, handling chopsticks can be a bit tricky at first, but with a little practice, your child will be able to wield them like a pro. Just cradle one chopstick in the curve between your thumb and index finger so that it rests on the tip of your ring finger. Set the second stick above the first, grasping it as you would a pencil. Now hold the bottom stick steady and move the top stick up and down. In time, you should be able to pick up even a single grain of rice.

Mexicali Pie

FamilyFun contributor Ken Haedrich has been making this colorful dish for 20 years, which says a lot about the enthusiastic response he always gets. If you're in a hurry, substitute a packet of taco seasoning for the spice mix.

FILLING

1 1/2   pounds ground beef

1   medium onion, chopped

1   green bell pepper, chopped

2   cloves garlic, minced

2   cups corn kernels

2   cans (14 1/2 ounces each) Mexican or chili-style diced tomatoes

SPICE MIX

2   teaspoons chili powder

1 1/2   teaspoons cumin

1   teaspoon ground coriander

1/4   teaspoon cayenne

1/2   teaspoon salt

1   tablespoon flour

CORN BREAD TOPPING

1   cup yellow cornmeal

1/2   cup flour

1 1/2   tablespoons sugar

2   teaspoons baking powder

1/4   teaspoon salt

1   large egg

1   cup milk

1/4   cup vegetable oil

1 Lightly oil a shallow, 3-quart casserole dish. Brown the ground beef in a large skillet, breaking it up with a wooden spoon. Use a slotted spoon to transfer the browned meat to the casserole dish. Drain all but about 3 tablespoons of the fat from the skillet.

KIDS' STEPS   Younger kids can measure and mix the spices and cornmeal topping. Older kids can brown the meat in the skillet.

2 Put the pan back on the heat and sauté the onion and bell pepper for 7 to 8 minutes. Meanwhile, combine the spice mix ingredients in a small bowl. Add the garlic and the spice mix, stirring all the while, then stir in the corn and tomatoes. Cover the pan and bring the mixture to a gentle boil, stirring occasionally. Transfer the vegetables to the casserole dish and stir together with the meat. Level the mixture with the back of the spoon.

3 Heat the oven to 400°. Sift the cornmeal, flour, sugar, baking powder, and salt into a medium mixing bowl. Whisk the egg, milk, and oil in a separate bowl. Add the dry mixture to the egg mixture and whisk until blended. Pour the batter over the filling and spread it out evenly. Bake until the topping is golden brown, about 22 minutes. For a festive finishing touch, serve the pie with a variety of chopped garnishes, such as avocado, black olives, lettuce, and scallions. Makes 8 to 10 servings.

Steak Fajitas

For families who like spice, this grilled dish delivers. For best results, use skirt steak for its superior taste and ability to absorb other flavors.

INGREDIENTS

- 2   to 2 ½ pounds skirt steak
-     Salt and pepper
- 2   tablespoons ground ginger
- 8   cloves garlic
- 2   limes, halved
- 2   to 3 tablespoons hot chili oil
- 10 to 12 tortillas
-     Guacamole or small red beans (optional)

1 Place the steak in a large, shallow casserole dish. Generously salt and pepper the exposed surfaces, then sprinkle with 1 tablespoon of the ginger. Mash the garlic into a paste — or mince it very fine — and spread half of it over the meat. Squeeze one of the limes over the meat, then drizzle on 1 to 1½ tablespoons of the chili oil, spreading it around with the back of a spoon. Turn the meat and repeat the procedure on the other side. (If you get any of the chili oil on your fingers, be sure to wash them thoroughly with warm, soapy water.) Cover the meat with plastic wrap and refrigerate for at least 2 hours, longer for more intense flavors.

2 Start your grill and cook the steak over low to moderate heat for about 6 to 7 minutes on each side, turning once, until done to your liking.

3 Remove the meat to a cutting board and let it rest for 5 minutes. Briefly warm the tortillas on the grill, or in the microwave or oven. Slice the meat thin, across the grain, and place several strips in a warmed tortilla. Add a spoonful of guacamole and/or beans. Roll up the tortilla and serve. Makes 5 to 6 servings.

KIDS' STEPS Kids can mix the marinade together and squeeze the lime on the meat.

Shepherd's Pie

POTATO TOPPING

- 6 cups peeled and chopped potatoes
- 2 teaspoons salt, plus more to taste
- 4 tablespoons butter, cut into pieces
- ½ cup sour cream
- ¼ to ½ cup milk
- 1½ cups grated white Cheddar cheese
  Paprika

FILLING

- 2 tablespoons butter
- 1 large onion, chopped
- 1 rib celery, chopped
- 1¼ pounds ground beef
- 1 clove garlic, minced
- 2 tablespoons flour
- 1 cup beef broth
- 1 cup diced canned tomatoes or crushed tomatoes in puree
- 1 teaspoon dried thyme
- ½ teaspoon dried rosemary
- 1½ cups corn kernels
- 1½ teaspoons Worcestershire sauce

Kids love this classic meat-and-potato pie. Layering the saucy ground beef, creamy mashed potatoes, and cheese will be as much fun for them as eating it.

1 Put the potatoes in a large pot and cover them with water. Add 2 teaspoons of salt to the water. Bring to a boil, uncovered, over high heat. Cook until you can slice through a potato chunk easily, about 10 minutes.

2 While the potatoes are cooking, start the filling. Melt the butter in a large skillet over medium heat. Sauté the onion and celery in the butter, stirring often, for about 5 to 6 minutes. Add the ground beef and break it up with a wooden spoon as it browns. Carefully drain the fat.

3 Lower the heat a bit, then stir the garlic and flour into the drained beef mixture. Stir in the beef broth, then the canned tomatoes, then the herbs, corn, and Worcestershire sauce.

4 Gently simmer the mixture for several minutes, partially covered, then add salt and pepper to taste. Transfer the mixture to a large buttered casserole dish. Heat the oven to 400°.

5 Drain the cooked potatoes and transfer them to a large mixing bowl. Scatter butter and sour cream over them, then mix the potatoes with an electric mixer, adding enough milk to make medium-soft mashed potatoes. Salt to taste.

6 Spoon the potatoes evenly over the filling. Sprinkle the cheese over the top, then sprinkle on some paprika. Bake on the center oven rack for about 20 minutes, until the top is golden brown. Cool for several minutes before serving. Makes 5 to 6 servings.

KIDS' STEPS Kids can mash the potatoes and layer the ingredients.

PREP TIME: **15 minutes** COOKING TIME: **about 1 hour**

Cheesy Meat Loaf

INGREDIENTS

1½ pounds lean ground beef

½ pound sweet pork sausage, casings removed

1 cup cubed Cheddar cheese

2 eggs

1 medium onion, finely chopped

½ green bell pepper, seeded and finely chopped

1 teaspoon salt

½ teaspoon black pepper

1 teaspoon celery salt

½ teaspoon paprika

1 cup milk

1 cup fine, dry bread crumbs

As a working mother of three, *FamilyFun* recipe tester Amy Hamel often makes this meat loaf with her children, who love its cheesy chunks.

1 Heat the oven to 350°. Line a large baking pan with oiled aluminum foil and set it aside.

2 Combine all of the ingredients in a large mixing bowl. Use your hands to blend everything together until it is evenly mixed.

3 Transfer the meat to the lined baking pan and form it into a long, fat loaf, about 10 by 5 inches. Bake the loaf for 60 to 70 minutes, until the center is cooked. Serve hot, warm, or cold. Makes 8 servings.

KIDS' STEPS Kids can mix the ingredients into the meat, making sure to wash their hands thoroughly afterward.

· ·

PREP TIME: **20 minutes** COOKING TIME: **20 minutes**

Sloppy Joes

INGREDIENTS

1 tablespoon vegetable oil

1 medium onion, diced

1 medium green bell pepper, diced

1 pound ground beef

1 can (8 ounces) tomato sauce

⅓ cup ketchup

2 teaspoons Worcestershire sauce

½ teaspoon chili powder

¼ teaspoon salt

¼ teaspoon ground pepper

6 rolls

A kid favorite to make or eat, there's something comforting about a sloppy joe, with its tangy, juicy meat spilling from the edges of a warm roll.

1 In a large frying pan, heat the oil over medium heat. Add the onion and diced pepper and sauté until soft. Add the ground beef, breaking it into pieces with a wooden spoon. Sauté until brown. Drain the fat.

2 Add the tomato sauce, ketchup, Worcestershire sauce, chili powder, salt, and pepper and stir well. Cook over low heat for 3 to 5 minutes. If you'd like the mixture to be even sloppier, add a few tablespoons of water.

3 While the meat mixture is simmering, heat the rolls, if desired. Arrange the bottom halves on a plate. Spoon the sloppy joe mixture on top of each half and cover each with the roll top. Makes 6 sandwiches.

KIDS' STEPS Older kids can sauté the vegetables and meat. Younger kids can spoon the mixture onto the open rolls.

PREP TIME: **about 15 minutes**   COOKING TIME: **1 hour**

Pork Arista and Pork Puppies

By taking some simple side steps, you can spin one pork roast into two very different recipes. The adult-friendly Pork Arista gets its great flavor from garlic and rosemary. The kid-friendly Pork Puppies, with the sweet tang of barbecue sauce, are wrapped in buttery crescent rolls.

INGREDIENTS

- 2 pounds boneless pork loin
- 1/4 cup bottled barbecue sauce (or blend 2 tablespoons each ketchup and brown sugar with 1/2 teaspoon each Worcestershire sauce and garlic powder)
- 2 tablespoons olive oil
- 1 tablespoon dried rosemary, crumbled
- 2 garlic cloves, peeled and slivered
- 1/2 cup dry white wine or vermouth (or the juice of 1 lemon plus enough water to make 1/2 cup)
- 1 tube crescent roll dough

KIDS' STEPS Kids can coat the loin with barbecue sauce for the Pork Puppies.

1 Heat the oven to 350°. Trim the fat from the pork. For the kids' meal, cut about a third of the meat from the thinner end or, if you have 2 pieces, use the smaller loin. Slice the kids' portion into 8 small hot dog-size pieces. Coat with barbecue sauce and put them on a baking sheet.

2 Rub the remaining loin with the olive oil, salt, and rosemary. Place it in a roasting pan. Using a sharp knife, cut slits in the meat all around and insert slivered garlic. Pour the wine or vermouth over the pork.

3 Place both pans of pork in the oven. Let the roast cook for 1 hour, basting it occasionally. Remove the kids' pork after 40 minutes and wrap the pieces in triangles of crescent dough. Bake them on the same baking sheet (covered with clean aluminum foil) until golden, about 12 minutes.

4 When the Pork Arista is done, let it sit for a couple of minutes to reabsorb some of its juices. Slice it thinly and serve with the remaining pan juices. Serves 2 adults and 2 kids.

Maple Pork Chops with Apples

Few pork recipes are as easy and tasty as this New England–style dish. If you can't find pork loin cutlets in your supermarket, you can use thin boneless pork chops instead.

INGREDIENTS

$\frac{1}{3}$ cup maple syrup

1 tablespoon spicy brown mustard

$\frac{1}{4}$ teaspoon salt

$\frac{1}{4}$ teaspoon pepper

$\frac{1}{4}$ cup bread crumbs

4 pork loin cutlets (about 1 pound)

2 teaspoons olive oil

$\frac{1}{2}$ cup apple cider

2 medium Golden Delicious or Granny Smith apples, each cored and cut into 16 wedges

1 In a small bowl, stir together the maple syrup, mustard, salt, and pepper until well combined.

2 Place the bread crumbs in a large ziplock bag, add the pork, then seal the bag and shake it to coat the cutlets.

3 Heat the oil in a large skillet over medium-high heat. Add the pork and cook it for 2 minutes on each side or until golden brown. Add the cider and apple wedges. Bring the cider to a boil, then reduce the heat and let it simmer uncovered for 5 to 7 minutes or until the pork is done.

4 Stir in the maple syrup mixture and cook the pork for 5 minutes more or until the pan sauces are thick and syrupy. Makes 4 servings.

KIDS' STEPS Kids can mix the maple syrup glaze and bread the pork chops.

FUN FOOD
Sea Dog

With a few simple cuts and a bed of seaweed (aka spinach pasta), you can transform a plain hot dog into a seafood dinner kids can't resist. First, cook the pasta (we used fettuccine) according to the package directions. For the octopus, cut slits along the length of a hot dog, stopping about 1 inch from the end, to create 8 dangling arms. Boil the hot dog as directed on the package. Set the hot dog atop a bed of seaweed noodles and add a mustard or ketchup face before serving.

PREP TIME: 30 minutes CHILLING TIME: 2 hours COOKING TIME: 20 minutes

Crispy Crab Cakes

Maybe it's that crab cakes look more like burgers than fish, or maybe it's that they have a delicious panfried flavor. But whatever the reason, they appeal to kids and adults alike.

INGREDIENTS

6	to 8 slices firm white bread
3	scallions, minced
2	tablespoons finely chopped red bell pepper
2	tablespoons chopped fresh parsley
1½	tablespoons chopped fresh dill
12	to 13 ounces crabmeat
1	egg
¼	cup mayonnaise
1	teaspoon Dijon mustard
2	teaspoons seafood seasoning (we used Old Bay brand)
½	teaspoon Worcestershire sauce
⅛	teaspoon salt
1	cup fine, dry bread crumbs
2	tablespoons butter for frying

1 Trim the crusts from the bread, then cut the trimmed slices into small cubes (altogether, you'll need 2½ cups of bread cubes). Put 1½ cups of the cubes into a large mixing bowl and set aside the rest.

2 Add the scallions, red bell pepper, parsley, dill, and crabmeat to the bowl. Use your hands to break up any lumps of crab, then toss the mixture until the ingredients are well combined.

3 In a small mixing bowl, lightly beat the egg. Add the mayonnaise, mustard, seafood seasoning, Worcestershire sauce, and salt. Whisk well to blend. Pour the sauce over the crab mixture, then stir with a wooden spoon until the new mixture clumps together.

4 Line a baking sheet with plastic wrap. Using your hands, shape the mixture into 6 large or 8 slightly smaller balls. Roll them in the reserved fresh bread cubes to coat and then place them atop the baking sheet. Flatten the balls slightly to form patties not quite 1 inch thick. Cover them with another piece of plastic wrap and chill them for 1 to 2 hours before frying.

5 When you're ready to fry the crab cakes, heat the oven to 300° and spread the dry bread crumbs on a plate. Melt 1 tablespoon of the butter in a medium skillet over medium heat. Working quickly so the butter doesn't burn, dredge half of the patties in the dry bread crumbs and fry them until they are nicely browned, about 3 to 6 minutes on each side. Transfer the cooked cakes to a baking pan and keep them in the warmed oven while you fry the second batch.

6 Before making the second batch, wipe out the pan with wadded paper towels (a parent's job) and then melt the other tablespoon of butter in it. Dredge and fry the remaining patties as before. Serve the crab cakes plain or on a lightly toasted roll with a slice of tomato, lettuce, and tartar sauce. Serves 4 to 6.

KIDS' STEPS Kids can cube the bread, flake the crabmeat, and shape the cakes.

PREP TIME: 15 minutes   COOKING TIME: about 10 minutes

Fast Fish Fingers

Simple and fun to make, these fish sticks are bound to become one of your family's favorite quick dinners. We used fillet of sole, but grouper and cod also work well.

QUICK SAUCE
Homemade Tartar Sauce

• • • • • • • • • • • • • • • • • •

Crown your fish fillet with this wholesome homemade topping. Just combine ¼ cup mayonnaise, ¼ cup sour cream, 1 tablespoon sweet pickle relish, 1 tablespoon finely chopped onion, 1 tablespoon finely chopped fresh parsley, and pepper (to taste) in a small mixing bowl. Stir briskly to blend. Makes about ¾ cup, enough for 6 servings.

INGREDIENTS

2	eggs
2	tablespoons water
	Salt and pepper to taste
1½	cups seasoned bread crumbs
3	tablespoons grated Parmesan cheese
2	pounds fillet of sole
¼	cup olive oil
1	lemon, cut into wedges
	Tartar sauce (optional)

1 In a bowl, beat the egg, water, salt, and pepper. In a separate bowl, mix the bread crumbs and Parmesan cheese.

2 Rinse the fish and cut it into 4- by 1-inch sticks. Lightly coat the sticks with the egg wash, then the bread crumbs.

3 Heat the oil in a large skillet over medium-high heat. Add the fish and cook until golden, about 3 minutes on each side. Remove the fish from the pan and set on a dish lined with paper towels to drain. Serve with lemon wedges and tartar sauce. Makes 6 servings.

KIDS' STEPS Kids can crack the eggs and bread the fish.

PREP TIME: **30 minutes**   COOKING TIME: **10 minutes**

Friendly Fish Fillets

Instead of being deep-fried, these flaky, golden fish fillets are coated with crackers and panfried in a small amount of canola oil. Serve them plain or create a fish sandwich with a hamburger bun, a slice of cheese, lettuce, and tartar sauce.

INGREDIENTS

³/₄ pound white fish (such as grouper or cod)

³/₄ cup flour

¹/₂ cup buttermilk

³/₄ cup crumbs from wheat crackers (such as Wheatsworth) ground in a food processor or crushed with a rolling pin

¹/₂ teaspoon salt

¹/₂ teaspoon pepper

¹/₄ teaspoon garlic powder

 1 tablespoon finely chopped fresh parsley

1¹/₂ tablespoons canola oil

 4 slices of cheese (optional)

1 Cut the fillets into 4 squares, each about 3½ by 3½ inches. Rinse them and dry them well on a paper towel.

2 Put the flour in one bowl and the buttermilk in another. Combine the wheat cracker crumbs, salt, pepper, garlic powder, and fresh parsley in a third, shallow bowl and blend well.

3 Dip each fish square into the flour, then the buttermilk, then the cracker crumb mixture. Set the pieces aside and heat the oil in a frying pan over medium-high heat.

4 Fry the fish squares in the pan until the bottoms are golden brown, about 4 minutes on each side. If you're making sandwiches, turn off the heat, lay the cheese slices over the hot fish squares, and cover the pan for a minute to melt the cheese. Makes 4 servings.

KIDS' STEPS Kids can crush the crackers with a rolling pin and mix up the crumb coating.

Plain and Simple Roast Chicken

MY GREAT IDEA
Candlelight Dinners
. . . .

"One dark winter evening, we discovered a new way to bring warmth and closeness to family dinners. My five-year-old son found an old box of half-burned candles, which I had put away because I thought romantic candlelight and small children didn't mix. My son insisted, however, on setting several on the table while my husband cooked dinner.

"As the family gathered, I lit the candles and dimmed the lights. The golden flames seemed to cast a magic spell — the kids spoke in hushed voices, and everyone inched closer to the table to stay inside the sphere of light. Instead of discussing the troubles of the day, we told stories and fantasized about life in a frontier cabin. And, for a while, we sat quietly and watched the flickering light reflecting in our frosty windowpanes.

"Now, the glow of candles and conversation often fills our house, the warmth lasting long after the flames have been blown out."

—Julie Dunlap
Columbia, Maryland

On a leisurely Sunday afternoon, pop a roasting chicken in the oven and it will be finished by dinnertime. Then your family can sit down to an old-fashioned dinner together. This recipe welcomes embellishments, such as the ones below.

INGREDIENTS

- 1   4- to 5-pound roasting chicken
-     Half a lemon
- 1   large onion, sliced
- 2   tablespoons olive oil
- 1   teaspoon thyme
- 1/2 teaspoon coarse salt
- 1/4 teaspoon pepper

1 Heat the oven to 400°. Remove the giblets, thoroughly rinse the chicken, and pat dry. Squeeze the juice from the lemon half over the chicken, then stuff the half into the cavity. Close the cavity with small skewers and tie the legs together with string.

2 Make a bed of onion slices in the bottom of a roasting pan and place the chicken, breast side up, on the onions. Drizzle with the olive oil, sprinkle with the thyme, salt, and pepper and bake for 1¼ to 1½ hours, basting frequently, until the juices from behind the leg run clear. Let rest 5 minutes, then carve. Serves 4 to 6.

VEGGIE ROAST CHICKEN
Surround the chicken with peeled carrots and pearl onions, unpeeled new potatoes, and whole mushrooms. Serve with the roasted vegetables on the side.

ORANGE-GINGER CHICKEN
Arrange orange slices on the bird, pour ½ cup orange juice over the top, and sprinkle with 1 tablespoon of peeled and minced fresh ginger.

APPLE-HAZELNUT CHICKEN
Place cored apple halves and peeled pearl onions in the roasting pan. Arrange apple slices on the bird and add a dash of cinnamon. Drizzle apple brandy over the bird for a fuller flavor. Ten minutes before the chicken is done, add 1 cup hazelnuts to the pan.

LEMON-ROSEMARY CHICKEN
Place lemon slices on the chicken and sprinkle generously with rosemary and a little olive oil.

STUFFED CHICKEN
Just before roasting, loosely stuff the chicken with your favorite stuffing mix. Increase the cooking time by 25 minutes.

KIDS' STEPS Kids can arrange the vegetables in the roasting pan and help tie the chicken legs together with string.

Easy Chicken Curry

The key to this quick curry's smooth and creamy texture is coconut milk, which can be found in the international food section of most supermarkets. To complete the meal, serve it over jasmine or basmati rice.

INGREDIENTS

- 1 1/2 tablespoons vegetable oil
- 1 medium onion, diced
- Salt
- 2 teaspoons curry powder
- 1 can (12 to 14 ounces) unsweetened coconut milk
- 1 cup canned diced tomatoes
- 2 tablespoons tomato paste
- 1 pound boneless, skinless chicken breasts, cut into 1-inch cubes
- 3 packed cups fresh baby spinach
- Jasmine or basmati rice (optional)

1 Heat the oil in a large skillet over medium heat. Add the onion and 1/4 teaspoon of salt. Cook the onion, stirring often, until soft (about 7 minutes). Add the curry powder and continue stirring for 1 minute more.

2 Stir in the coconut milk, tomatoes, and tomato paste. Continue cooking the mixture, stirring occasionally, for 5 minutes or until the sauce thickens slightly.

3 Add the chicken, stir well, and cook for 5 to 6 minutes or until the meat is cooked through. Add the spinach and cook, stirring occasionally, until wilted, about 3 minutes. Add more salt to taste. Serve warm, over rice. Makes 4 servings.

KIDS' STEPS Older kids can sauté the onions. Younger kids can wash and measure the spinach.

Chicken and Dumplings

When she was a kid, *FamilyFun* reader Julie Banal of Fergus Falls, Minnesota, would often find this savory meal simmering on her grandmother's stove. "The more of it you ate," says Julie, "the more she loved you." Julie says it's a real treat cooking this dish with her own children now.

CHICKEN

2	tablespoons vegetable oil
3	to 4 pounds chicken pieces (legs, breasts, thighs)
1	small onion, chopped
2	ribs celery, thinly sliced
3	cups plus ½ cup water
1	bay leaf
3	chicken bouillon cubes
1	teaspoon salt
	Black pepper to taste
5	medium carrots, peeled and sliced
⅓	cup flour

DUMPLINGS

1½	cups flour
2	teaspoons baking powder
¼	teaspoon salt
1	tablespoon chopped fresh parsley
⅔	cup milk
1	egg
1	tablespoon vegetable oil

1 Heat the 2 tablespoons of oil in a large Dutch oven or other large saucepan. Add the chicken pieces and brown them on each side for 2 minutes.

2 Stir in the onion and celery. Sauté briefly, then add 3 cups of water, the bay leaf, bouillon, salt, and pepper. Bring to a boil, then reduce the heat and simmer, covered, for 30 minutes.

3 Remove the chicken and add the carrots to the pot. Cover and simmer for 10 minutes or until the carrots are tender. Meanwhile, remove the chicken meat from the bones.

4 Whisk together the ⅓ cup of flour and the remaining ½ cup of water in a medium bowl until smooth. Add the mixture and the chicken meat to the simmering saucepan. Cover and continue to simmer.

KIDS' STEPS Kids can stir up the dumpling mix and spoon it (with supervision) into the broth.

5 To prepare the dumplings, combine the flour, baking powder, salt, and fresh parsley in a large bowl. Make a well in the dry mixture and add the milk, egg, and oil. Stir briskly to make a batter. For each dumpling, spoon a rounded tablespoon of batter into the simmering broth. Cover and simmer for another 13 to 15 minutes, without stirring. Ladle into wide soup bowls and serve hot. Makes 5 to 6 servings.

Potato Chip Chicken Fingers

These irresistible fingers get their crunch not from deep-frying but from potato chips. Experiment with chip flavors, from barbecue to sour cream and chive.

KIDS' STEPS Kids can beat the egg, crush the chips, and coat the chicken pieces.

INGREDIENTS

- 1 to 1½ pounds whole boneless, skinless chicken breast
- 5 to 6 ounces potato chips (plain, barbecue, or sour cream) or tortilla chips
- ½ teaspoon salt
- ½ teaspoon pepper
- 1 egg
- 2 tablespoons milk
  Carrot curls (optional)
  Grape or cherry tomatoes (optional)

1 Heat the oven to 400°. Cut the chicken into finger-size pieces. Thread the pieces onto soaked wooden skewers (if desired).

2 Fill a large ziplock bag with the potato chips, salt, and pepper. Seal the bag, then crush the chips with the back of a wooden spoon or a rolling pin. In a medium bowl, beat the egg and milk. Dip the chicken pieces into the egg mixture, then put them in the bag and shake gently to coat.

3 Place the chicken pieces on an ungreased cookie sheet and bake for 20 minutes, flipping once. Serve with barbecue or honey mustard dipping sauce (below) or salsa. Makes 4 to 6 servings.

BARBECUE DIPPING SAUCE
In a small bowl, mix together ½ cup ketchup, 2 tablespoons maple syrup, 1 tablespoon soy sauce, ½ teaspoon cinnamon, ¼ teaspoon ground ginger, and, if you like, a dash of hot pepper sauce until well blended. Cover and refrigerate until ready to use.

HONEY MUSTARD DIPPING SAUCE
In a small bowl, mix ¼ cup Dijon mustard, 1 tablespoon honey, and 1 tablespoon water with a fork until smooth.

PREP TIME: about 15 minutes   COOKING TIME: about 15 minutes

Easy Chicken Cutlets

These cutlets are an easy recipe for a parent and child to prepare together. They taste great dipped in our honey mustard sauce (see opposite page), or topped with marinara sauce and mozzarella cheese to make Chicken Parmesan.

INGREDIENTS

4	boneless, skinless chicken breasts (about 6 ounces each)
2/3	cup fine, dry bread crumbs
1/3	cup freshly grated Parmesan cheese
2	teaspoons dried basil
1	teaspoon dried oregano
1/2	teaspoon salt
1/8	teaspoon pepper
1	egg, beaten
2	tablespoons milk
1/2	cup flour
2	to 4 tablespoons olive oil for frying

1 Rinse the chicken breasts under running water, then place them on a double layer of paper towels and blot them dry. (Be sure to wash your hands well in warm soapy water immediately after handling raw chicken; do the same for any cutting boards or utensils that the meat comes into contact with.)

2 Place 2 of the chicken breasts inside a large, heavy-duty plastic freezer bag. Partially seal the bag, leaving a slight gap so air can escape. Using a rolling pin or the smooth head of a tenderizing mallet, pound the meat in even strokes, working from the center out (be careful not to tear the plastic), to a uniform thickness of about ⅓ inch. Repeat this process with the remaining chicken in a new plastic bag.

3 Combine the bread crumbs, Parmesan cheese, basil, oregano, salt, and pepper in a shallow bowl. Stir them to mix. In a separate shallow bowl or pie plate, beat together the egg and milk. Set both of the bowls aside.

KIDS' STEPS Kids can pound the chicken, prepare the bowls for dredging, and bread the cutlets.

4 Spread the flour on a plate. Arrange the breading ingredients in assembly-line fashion in this order: cutlets, flour, egg mixture, crumb mixture, empty plate. Bread the cutlets as shown below.

5 Set a large skillet over medium-high heat and pour in enough olive oil to coat the bottom of the pan. Heat the oil for 2 to 3 minutes, then add the cutlets. (If your pan isn't large enough to cook 4 chicken breasts at once, cook them in batches rather than overcrowd the pan.) Fry each side for 2½ to 3 minutes, turning once, until the chicken is browned and cooked through. Remove the cutlets from the heat and serve. Makes 4 servings.

TEACHING KIDS TO COOK
How to Bread Cutlets

Working one piece at a time, dredge both sides of the cutlet in the flour, knocking off the excess.

Dip both sides of the floured cutlet in the egg mixture.

Coat both sides of the cutlet with the crumb mixture. Repeat the process with the remaining pieces.

Turkey Potpie

Show your child how to turn leftover turkey into this savory hot dish that's on everyone's list of favorite comfort foods.

INGREDIENTS

4	tablespoons butter
1	medium onion, chopped
1	rib celery, chopped
¼	cup flour
1¼	cups chicken or turkey stock
1¼	cups milk
1	teaspoon crumbled or powdered dried sage
¾	teaspoon dried thyme
	Salt and pepper to taste
2	cups diced cooked turkey
2	cups cooked mixed vegetables
	Pie dough, store-bought or homemade

GLAZE

1	egg yolk
1	tablespoon milk

1 Melt the butter in a large sauté pan over medium-low heat. Stir in the onion and celery. Cover the pan and gently sweat the vegetables (cook them, covered, over medium-low heat) for about 8 minutes, stirring occasionally. Then stir in the flour. Increase the heat slightly and continue to cook and stir the mixture for 1 more minute.

2 Add the stock to the pan, whisking to evenly blend all of the ingredients. As the stock starts to thicken, whisk in the milk, sage, thyme, salt, and pepper. Depending on the saltiness of the stock you've used, you will likely need about ½ teaspoon of salt. Start with a little less, then taste the sauce and add more if needed.

3 Stir in the turkey and vegetables and simmer the mixture, stirring often, for 2 minutes. Remove the pan from the heat.

4 Generously butter a 2-quart round, shallow casserole (about 8½ to 9½ inches with sloping sides). Transfer the filling to the casserole and smooth the top. Let the filling cool for about 15 minutes. Meanwhile, heat the oven to 400°.

5 While the oven heats, prepare the dough for the top crust. Put a sheet of waxed paper (about 12 inches long) on your work counter and lightly flour it. Put the dough on the waxed paper, dust it and your rolling pin with flour, then roll it into an 11-inch disk. Start in the middle and push the pin out toward the edge of the disk, turning the paper as needed to roll the dough evenly.

6 Invert the crust, with the paper, so it is centered atop the filling, as shown. Peel away the paper and fit the edge of the crust into the dish. In a small bowl, whisk the egg yolk and milk for the glaze. Lightly brush the glaze onto the crust, then use a fork to poke 4 or 5 steam vents in the pastry.

7 Bake on the center oven rack until well browned, about 40 minutes. Slide an aluminum foil-lined baking sheet onto the shelf below the pie to catch any spills. Transfer the potpie to a cooling rack and cool for 10 minutes before serving. Makes 6 servings.

KIDS' STEPS Younger kids can butter the casserole dish and glaze the crust. Older kids can sauté the vegetables and fill the casserole dish.

Garlic Bread Galore

• • • • • • • • • • • • • • • • • •

For restaurant-quality garlic bread, follow these easy recipes.

GARLIC BUTTER
Mash 4 tablespoons of room temperature butter with 1 to 2 crushed garlic cloves. For melted garlic butter, microwave the butter, then add the crushed garlic cloves. Mix in fresh basil or parsley to give the butter extra color and flavor.

NOTHING FANCY GARLIC BREAD
Cut a loaf of French bread into 1-inch slices (but not all the way through the bottom crust) and spread each slice with garlic butter. Wrap in foil and bake in a 350° oven for 5 minutes or until heated through.

CRISPY GARLIC BREAD
Brush both sides of 1-inch rounds of French bread with melted garlic butter. Place on a cookie sheet and broil each side until golden.

GARLIC STICKS
Cut a loaf of French bread the long way and spread with garlic butter or brush with melted garlic butter. Broil, cut side up, until brown. Cut into 1-inch slices.

PREP TIME: 35 minutes   **COOKING TIME:** 40 minutes

Spaghetti and Meatballs

What's better than sitting down to a steaming plate of freshly cooked al dente pasta, homemade meatballs, and rich tomato sauce? Why, making it, of course.

MEATBALLS
- ¾ pound ground beef
- ¼ pound ground sweet or hot Italian sausage
- 3 tablespoons grated Parmesan cheese
- 2 tablespoons bread crumbs
- 2 teaspoons onion powder or 2 tablespoons finely chopped onion
- ½ teaspoon dried basil
- ½ teaspoon salt
- 2 garlic cloves, minced
- 1 egg
- 2 to 3 tablespoons olive oil

TOMATO SAUCE
- 1 medium onion, finely chopped
- 3 tablespoons finely grated carrot (about ½ small carrot)
- 1½ tablespoons olive oil
- 2 garlic cloves, minced
- 1 can (28 ounces) crushed tomatoes
- Salt to taste

PASTA
- 1 pound spaghetti
- Parmesan cheese

1 To make the meatballs, mix together all the ingredients except the olive oil and form into 1-inch balls (the size of small walnuts). In a large skillet, brown the meatballs in the oil until cooked through, about 8 to 10 minutes.

2 To make the tomato sauce, sauté the onion and carrot in the olive oil for 3 to 4 minutes over medium-high heat. Add the garlic and cook for another minute. Add the tomatoes and reduce the heat to medium, cooking another 10 to 15 minutes. Add salt to taste, then toss in the meatballs.

3 While the meatballs gently simmer in the sauce, bring a pot of water to a boil for the pasta. Cook until the pasta is al dente, or slightly chewy. Fill individual bowls with the cooked pasta and add the sauce. Serve with Parmesan cheese. Makes 24 to 30 meatballs and 3 cups of tomato sauce, enough for 4 servings.

OPTION: You can bake the meatballs instead of sautéing them. Arrange them on a lightly oiled baking sheet and bake at 350°, turning once or twice, until brown and cooked through, about 20 minutes.

KIDS' STEPS   Younger kids can roll the meatballs (washing their hands after handling the raw meat). Older kids can sauté the meatballs and the vegetables for the sauce.

Cheese Ravioli

Because it's so easy to make, fresh pasta is a great family cooking project. Plus, it has a wonderfully delicate texture you just can't find in store-bought varieties. If you plan to make fresh pasta on a regular basis, consider a pasta machine to achieve optimal thickness.

PASTA

1 1/2	cups flour
1/4	teaspoon salt, plus more for the cooking water
2	eggs
1	tablespoon water
2	teaspoons olive oil, plus 1 tablespoon for the cooking water
1	quart tomato-based pasta sauce

FILLING

3/4	cup ricotta cheese
1/2	cup freshly grated Parmesan cheese
1	egg yolk
2	tablespoons chopped fresh parsley
1/8	teaspoon salt
	Ground pepper to taste
	Pinch of nutmeg

1 Combine the flour and salt in a large mixing bowl and toss. Make a well in the center of the flour and add the eggs, water, and 2 teaspoons of oil. Blend the liquids with a fork. Using your hand, gradually mix the flour into the well by pulling it into the liquid with quick strokes. The dough may stick to your fingers, but keep blending until it forms a firm, if somewhat shaggy, mass. On a surface dusted with flour, knead the dough for 3 to 4 minutes, then place it in a plastic bag and set it aside for 20 minutes.

2 While the dough rests, combine all of the filling ingredients in a medium bowl and mix well.

3 Remove the dough from the plastic bag and dust it with flour. Flatten the dough with your hands, then, for hand rolling, dust it lightly with flour and roll it as thinly as you can. Go easy with the flour — too much will dry out the pasta.

If you're using a pasta machine, feed the dough through the rollers. Start with the thickest setting, then decrease the thickness one notch with each progressive pass until the dough is almost paper-thin.

4 Using a 2- to 2¼-inch biscuit or cookie cutter (or a clean tomato paste can), cut out as many dough circles as you can. Reroll the scraps and cut out more. Loosely cover the dough with plastic wrap to prevent drying.

5 For each ravioli, put a teaspoon of filling in the center of one circle, then lightly dampen the perimeter with water. Dampen the edge of a second circle and place it atop the first one. Pinch the edges together to seal, then place them on a flour-dusted baking sheet and keep them loosely covered with plastic wrap until cooking time.

6 Carefully place the ravioli in a large pot of boiling water to which 1 tablespoon of olive oil and 2 teaspoons of salt have been added. Boil gently for about 4 minutes (fresh pasta cooks quickly), then drain and blot the ravioli lightly with paper towels. Serve at once with warmed pasta sauce. Makes 4 to 5 servings.

KIDS' STEPS Kids can roll the dough and cut out ravioli shapes.

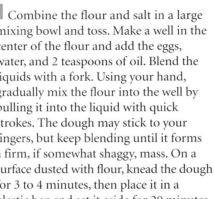

Perfect Pesto

When the basil in your garden is at full capacity, have the kids pinch off the leaves and help you whip up this batch of nutty, fragrant pesto to mix into pasta or chunks of sautéed white-meat chicken.

INGREDIENTS

- 2 or 3 whole garlic cloves, peeled
- ¼ cup pine nuts or walnut pieces
- ½ teaspoon salt
- 2 cups packed fresh basil leaves
- ½ cup olive oil
- ⅔ cup freshly grated Parmesan cheese

1 Combine the garlic, nuts, and ½ teaspoon of salt in the bowl of a food processor and process until they are finely chopped.

2 Add the basil and oil and process again until the herb is finely chopped, stopping to scrape the sides of the bowl several times.

3 Transfer the mixture to a bowl, then stir in the cheese. Makes about 5 servings with 1 pound of cooked pasta.

TIP: It's okay to make pesto in advance; just keep it chilled and then bring it back to room temperature before you're ready to toss it into your freshly cooked pasta (we suggest kid-favorite angel hair) or chicken.

KIDS' STEPS Kids can wash and stem the basil leaves and put the ingredients in the food processor.

Wisconsin Mac and Cheese

INGREDIENTS

Butter for greasing the dish

12   ounces elbow macaroni

1   tablespoon olive oil

1   cup heavy cream

1   cup half-and-half (or light cream)

2   egg yolks

1/2   teaspoon ground nutmeg

2   cups grated extra-sharp Cheddar cheese

2   cups grated Fontina cheese

2   cups grated Parmesan cheese

2   teaspoons Worcestershire sauce

1/2   teaspoon white pepper

1   cup bread crumbs

Sure, you can make this staple of every kid's diet from a box. But taking the time to make it from scratch offers rewards of rich flavor you never dreamed you'd find in such a common dish. We find the combination of Cheddar, Fontina, and Parmesan cheeses offers the best flavor and texture.

1 Heat the oven to 400°. Grease a 3- or 4-quart casserole dish and set it aside.

2 Bring a pot of lightly salted water to a boil. Add the macaroni and cook until tender but still firm to the bite. Drain well and transfer to the prepared baking dish. Toss with the olive oil.

3 Combine the cream, half-and-half, egg yolks, and nutmeg in a medium saucepan. Place over medium-low heat and add 1½ cups each Cheddar, Fontina, and Parmesan cheese. Stir gently and cook until the cheeses are melted and the sauce is smooth, about 5 to 10 minutes. Do not boil. Season with Worcestershire sauce and white pepper.

4 Pour the sauce over the macaroni and stir until it is completely coated. Sprinkle the remaining cheese on top. Bake until the sauce bubbles and the edges are lightly browned, about 15 minutes.

5 Remove from the oven. Set the oven to broil. Sprinkle the bread crumbs evenly over the macaroni and broil for a minute or until the top is golden brown (watching carefully). Serve immediately. Makes 6 to 8 servings.

KIDS' STEPS Older kids can grate the cheeses. Younger kids can mix the melted cheese into the cooked macaroni.

Kids' First Mac and Cheese

INGREDIENTS

1   pound elbow macaroni

Butter for greasing the dish

3   cups half-and-half

12   to 18 slices American or Cheddar cheese

12   Ritz crackers

Salt, pepper, and paprika to taste

Here's a simple version of the savory classic that goes together layer by layer, making it fun for kids to help prepare as well as eat.

1 Bring a pot of lightly salted water to a boil. Add the macaroni and cook until tender but still firm. Drain well.

2 Meanwhile, heat the oven to 350° and grease a 13- by 9-inch baking pan or a large casserole dish.

3 Spoon a third of the pasta into the pan, then pour in 1 cup of the half-and-half and cover it all with 4 to 6 slices of cheese. Add two more layers of pasta, half-and-half, and cheese.

4 Place the crackers in a ziplock bag and crush. Add the salt, pepper, and paprika, then sprinkle the crumbs on top of the pasta and cheese. Bake until bubbly, about 30 to 40 minutes. Makes 6 to 8 servings.

KIDS' STEPS Kids can help layer the cheese and pasta and crush the crackers for the topping.

PREP TIME: **5 minutes**   COOKING TIME: **20 minutes**

Penne Alfredo with Peas and Smoked Fish

Penne with a basic Alfredo sauce for the kids can be easily dressed up with smoked trout or salmon for the grown-ups, resulting in a savory blend sophisticated enough to serve to company.

KIDS' STEPS Younger kids can measure the ingredients. Older kids can help cook the Alfredo sauce.

INGREDIENTS

- 1 pound penne
- 1 cup frozen petite peas
- 4 tablespoons butter
- 1 cup heavy cream
- 2/3 cup freshly grated Parmesan cheese
- 1/2 teaspoon salt
- Pinch of nutmeg (freshly ground, if available)
- 1 to 1 1/2 pounds smoked trout or salmon fillets, boned and flaked

1 Boil the penne according to the directions on the package and, in the last minute of boiling, add the frozen peas. While the pasta cooks, begin preparing the Alfredo sauce (step 2). Strain the cooked penne and peas. If they're ready before the sauce, toss them back into the pot with an extra 2 tablespoons of butter, stir, and keep them warm.

2 In a medium pot, bring the butter and cream to a boil and immediately lower the heat so the mixture gently simmers. Cook the sauce, stirring occasionally, for about 4 minutes or until it leaves a thick coating on the spoon. Stir in the grated cheese, salt, and nutmeg.

3 Dish out the kids' penne and peas and top it with Alfredo sauce. If your kids usually go for seconds, reserve some extra penne and plain sauce on the side before preparing the adult dishes.

4 To the remaining sauce, add a few twists of black pepper, the smoked fish, and the rest of the penne and peas. Toss gently to coat. Serves 2 adults and 2 kids.

PASTA   155

Skillet Lasagna

For food writer Helen Wolt, dinner often begins with a mad dash through the supermarket at 4:30 p.m. Fortunately, her skillet lasagna recipe is quick to assemble. While the lasagna is simmering, Helen warms breadsticks and tosses a salad.

INGREDIENTS

1 ¼	cups ricotta cheese
¼	cup water
½	teaspoon salt
¼	cup grated Parmesan cheese
1 ½	cups shredded mozzarella cheese
1	pound lean ground beef
1	medium zucchini, diced
24	ounces (3 cups) tomato-based pasta sauce
6	oven-ready lasagna noodles

1 In a medium bowl, mix together the ricotta cheese, water, salt, Parmesan cheese, and ½ cup of the mozzarella cheese. Set the mixture aside.

2 Brown the beef in a large skillet set over medium-high heat until it's no longer pink, breaking up any clumps with a wooden spoon. Drain the fat, then add the zucchini and 2 cups of the tomato sauce. Reduce the heat to medium-low.

3 Top the mixture with 2 lasagna noodles. Break 2 more noodles into medium-size pieces and fill in the edges of the pan. Gently spread the cheese mixture over the noodles. (The noodles may begin to curl in the skillet, but the cheeses will hold them down.) Lay on the 2 remaining noodles. Pour the rest of the sauce into the skillet and spread it evenly, then sprinkle on the remaining cup of mozzarella cheese.

4 Cover the skillet and simmer the lasagna over medium-low heat until the noodles are tender, about 20 minutes. Remove the skillet from the heat and let the lasagna cool for 5 minutes. Makes 6 servings.

KIDS' STEPS Kids can measure and mix the ricotta cheese filling and, with supervision, layer the noodles in the skillet.

PREP TIME: 40 minutes   **COOKING TIME:** 1 hour 10 minutes

Lasagna Rolls

A rich, satisfying dish, these rolls can be prepared in two sizes — one for a family meal and a smaller one for a potluck. They freeze nicely, too, so double the recipe if you like.

INGREDIENTS

24	ounces (3 cups) tomato-based pasta sauce
1/2	small yellow onion, chopped
5	ounces ground turkey
5	ounces ground Italian sausage
1/4	teaspoon salt
1/8	teaspoon pepper
1/2	teaspoon Italian seasoning
1	egg
1 1/2	cups ricotta cheese
1/4	cup grated Parmesan cheese
1 1/2	cups shredded mozzarella cheese
6	lasagna noodles (plus extra to allow for breakage)

1 Heat the oven to 350°. Coat the bottom of a 7- by 11-inch pan with cooking spray, then 1/2 cup of the sauce.

2 In a large saucepan, brown the onion, turkey, and sausage. Drain any fat, then add half the remaining sauce, the salt, pepper, and Italian seasoning. Bring to a boil and simmer for 15 minutes.

3 In a bowl, lightly beat the egg, then stir in the ricotta, Parmesan, and 1 cup of the mozzarella until thoroughly mixed.

4 Boil the noodles until tender, then rinse in cold water. Lay out a strip of noodle and spread about 2 tablespoons of the cheese mixture along the entire length. (To make smaller, potluck-size servings, cut the noodle in half lengthwise before spreading on the cheese.) Spread about 2 tablespoons of the meat mixture on top of the cheese. Roll up the noodle and place it (frilled edge up for the smaller ones) in the prepared pan. Repeat with the remaining noodles.

5 Pour the remaining sauce over the rolls and sprinkle the top of each with the rest of the mozzarella. Cover the pan with aluminum foil and bake for 30 minutes. Remove the foil and bake for 15 minutes more. Serves 6 (12 for a potluck).

KIDS' STEPS Kids can fill and roll up the lasagna noodles.

KITCHEN FUN
Kids' Cooking Party

Two things kids crave are food and fun. You can combine both these loves with a kids' lasagna cooking party.

Start by sending out invitations written on blank recipe cards. When the kids arrive, hand them paper chef hats and invite them to cook up their own lasagnas.

Give each child a disposable loaf pan (the type with plastic tops are best for sending home leftovers) and have them write their names in permanent marker on the side. Lay out all the lasagna ingredients in the middle of the table — precooked lasagna noodles, precooked meats (sausage and ground beef), tomato sauce, and cheeses (mozzarella, ricotta, and Parmesan) — and let each child build a customized lasagna, starting with sauce on the bottom of the pan so the noodles won't stick.

Put the pans on a cookie sheet and bake at 300° for about 20 minutes or until the ingredients are warm and the cheese has melted. Serve the lasagnas slightly cooled and let the kids eat right out of the pans.

Pasta Primavera with Shrimp

Baby carrots and sugar snap peas give this simplified primavera plenty of kid appeal, but if your family prefers other fresh vegetables, such as asparagus, green beans, or zucchini, they'll work well too.

INGREDIENTS

1½ cups baby carrots, trimmed

2 cups sugar snap peas

3 cups penne

1 tablespoon olive oil

32 or so (about 8 ounces) medium peeled shrimp, fresh or thawed

¼ teaspoon salt

¼ teaspoon freshly ground black pepper

2 garlic cloves, minced

¼ cup chicken broth

⅓ cup heavy cream

1 tablespoon fresh lemon juice

¼ cup freshly grated Parmesan cheese

⅓ cup chopped fresh parsley

1 Bring 2 quarts of water to a boil in a large pot. Add the carrots and let them simmer for 1½ minutes. Add the snap peas and simmer for another minute. Use a slotted spoon to transfer the vegetables to a bowl. Now, cook the pasta in the boiling water according to the package directions. Drain the pasta well.

2 Heat the oil in a large skillet over medium-high heat. Add the shrimp and cook them, stirring often, for 2 minutes. Add the carrots, peas, salt, pepper, and garlic and continue cooking for another minute, stirring often.

3 Stir in the chicken broth, scraping the pan to loosen any browned bits. Then stir in the cream and lemon juice and cook for 1 minute. Add the pasta and grated cheese, stirring well to coat. Remove the pan from the heat and stir in the parsley. Serve warm. Makes 4 to 6 servings.

KIDS' STEPS Kids can wash and trim the snap peas. Older kids can sauté the shrimp and vegetables.

Pasta with Maple Mustard Chicken

Linda Hopkins, founder of Les Petites Gourmettes cooking school for children, believes that kids will be more likely to try new foods if they've helped prepare them. She and her students took a field trip to the supermarket to learn how to compare prices and select unfamiliar ingredients, such as the fresh herbs and garlic in this savory dish.

INGREDIENTS

- 2 tablespoons olive oil
- 1 large garlic clove, minced
- 1 tablespoon chopped fresh rosemary
- 1 tablespoon chopped fresh chives
- 1 tablespoon apple cider vinegar
- 2 1/2 tablespoons maple syrup
- 2 tablespoons spicy brown mustard
- 2 skinless, boneless chicken breast halves (about 1 pound)
- 1 cup chicken stock
- 3/4 cup roasted red peppers, diced
- 1/4 cup sun-dried tomatoes, chopped
- 1/4 pound snow peas, stemmed and lightly steamed
- 1/2 pound penne, cooked

1 Heat 1 tablespoon of the olive oil in a small saucepan over medium heat. Sauté the garlic in the oil for just 30 seconds (if the garlic overcooks, it will taste bitter). Add the herbs and vinegar and cook for 30 seconds more. Pour the mixture into a small bowl to cool, then whisk in the maple syrup and mustard.

2 Slice the chicken pieces in half and place in a large ziplock bag. Pour in the marinade and turn the meat once to coat it. Cover the bowl and chill the chicken for at least 1 hour or overnight.

3 Heat the remaining tablespoon of oil in a large skillet over medium-high heat. Meanwhile, remove the chicken from the glass dish, saving the marinade, and sprinkle it with salt and pepper. Add the chicken to the skillet and sauté it for 2 minutes on each side to seal in the juices. Reduce the heat to medium and continue heating the chicken until it is cooked through and browned, about 6 minutes. Transfer the chicken to a cutting board, let it rest for 5 minutes, then cut it into bite-size cubes.

4 To deglaze (that is, to use the cooking juices that have browned in the skillet to make a glaze), start by adding 1/2 cup of the chicken stock to the skillet and simmering it until it reduces by half. Add the remaining chicken stock and the reserved marinade and bring the mixture to a boil. Continue cooking at a simmer until the liquid has thickened, 5 or more minutes.

5 Combine the chicken, red peppers, sun-dried tomatoes, snow peas, and cooked penne in a large bowl. Pour in the sauce and toss to combine. Makes 4 servings.

KIDS' STEPS Older kids can chop the herbs and vegetables. Younger kids can sprinkle the chicken with salt and pepper.

TIP: Mincing garlic releases its intense flavor. To mince a peeled clove, slice it thinly vertically then horizontally.

PREP TIME: **about 10 minutes**   COOKING TIME: **about 20 minutes**

Pad Thai

Thailand's equivalent of spaghetti and meatballs, pad thai is a sweet, tangy, crunchy noodle dish perfect for introducing kids to international foods.

INGREDIENTS

- 7 ounces wide rice noodles
- ¼ cup fish sauce (available in the international foods aisle)
- 2 tablespoons sugar
- 3 tablespoons peanut or vegetable oil
- 1 tablespoon soy sauce
- Juice of 1 lime
- Pinch of red pepper flakes (optional)
- 7 ounces tofu (extra firm), dried well and cut into ½-inch cubes (optional)
- 2 eggs, lightly beaten
- 1 garlic clove, minced
- ½ cup chopped cooked shrimp
- 2 cups bean sprouts
- ½ cup chopped dry-roasted peanuts (optional)
- ½ cup chopped cilantro leaves, lightly packed (optional)

1 Soak the noodles in hot water according to the package directions. Combine the fish sauce, sugar, 2 tablespoons of the oil, soy sauce, lime juice, and the red pepper flakes in a small bowl and set the mixture aside.

2 Heat the remaining tablespoon of oil in a large pan over medium-high heat. Sauté the tofu cubes until golden brown, about 7 to 8 minutes, then remove them from the pan and set them aside. Reduce the heat to medium-low and cook the beaten eggs (you can use the same pan), breaking up any large pieces. When they're done, set the eggs aside with the tofu cubes.

3 Sauté the garlic and shrimp for about 30 seconds, then add the fish sauce mixture and the drained noodles to the pan. Add the tofu cubes, eggs, and bean sprouts, stirring gently until everything is thoroughly heated. Remove to a serving dish and garnish with the peanuts and cilantro, if desired. Makes 8 cups.

 **KIDS' STEPS** Kids can measure and mix the sauce and drain the noodles.

Peanut Butter Noodles

This nutty noodle dish is everything a kid could want: sweet, salty, crunchy, and slathered in peanut butter. The thin noodles cook quickly and are served cold, making this a perfect light supper.

INGREDIENTS

- 1 pound linguini, angel hair pasta, or soba noodles
- ½ cup creamy peanut butter
- 5 tablespoons rice wine vinegar
- 5 tablespoons sesame oil
- 4 tablespoons soy sauce
- 2 teaspoons peeled, grated fresh ginger
- 1 small garlic clove, crushed

1 Cook the noodles according to the package directions, then drain and rinse with cold water.

2 In a large bowl, blend together the peanut butter, vinegar, sesame oil, soy sauce, ginger, and garlic. Add the noodles or pasta, toss well, then garnish with the toppings. Serve at room temperature. Makes 4 to 6 servings.

OPTIONAL TOPPINGS Grated carrot, scallion (sliced into rounds), cucumber (peeled, seeded, and thinly sliced), toasted sesame seeds, and/or chopped peanuts.

KIDS' STEPS Kids can measure and mix the ingredients and crush garlic in the garlic press.

Homemade Pizza Pie

No matter how you slice it, pizza rules. And although parlor pies are great, once in a while it's a real treat for kids to make one from scratch.

DOUGH

- 1 ⅓ cups lukewarm water
- 1 package (¼ ounce) active dry yeast
- 1 teaspoon sugar
- 1 ½ tablespoons olive oil
- 1 ½ teaspoons salt
- 3 ¼ to 3 ½ cups flour

TOPPING

- 2 tablespoons olive oil
- 1 ½ cups of your favorite tomato-based pasta sauce
- 1 ½ cups grated white Cheddar cheese
- 1 cup grated mozzarella cheese
- Toppers, such as sliced or chopped cooked meats and/or vegetables

1 Pour ⅓ cup of the water into a small bowl and sprinkle the yeast over it. Proof the yeast by stirring the sugar into it with a fork and letting it set for 5 to 8 minutes to see if the liquid turns frothy. If it does, it's active; if not, you'll need to start again with a fresh package of yeast.

2 Combine the dissolved yeast with the remaining water, the oil, and the salt in a large bowl. Stir well. Add 2 cups of the flour and beat well by hand for 100 strokes. Let the mixture rest for 5 minutes.

3 Add the remaining flour ⅓ cup at a time, beating well each time. When the dough is firm enough to knead, turn it out onto a floured surface. With floured hands, knead for 7 to 8 minutes, until smooth and elastic.

4 Put the dough in a large, lightly oiled bowl, turning it once to coat both sides. Cover the bowl with plastic wrap and set it in a warm, draft-free spot until the dough doubles in bulk, about an hour.

5 Punch down the dough several times, then knead it on a lightly floured surface for 1 minute. Divide it in half, knead each half into a ball, then set them on the floured surface. Cover them with plastic wrap and let them rest for 10 minutes. Lightly oil 1 large or 2 medium-large baking sheets, then dust them with cornmeal.

6 Once the dough has rested, roll or pat each ball into a ¼-inch thick circle. If the dough springs back as you work with it, let it rest for another 2 minutes.

7 Carefully lift each dough circle onto a baking sheet. If you're baking both on a single sheet, be sure to leave some room between them. Loosely cover the crusts with plastic wrap and let them rest for 10 minutes. Heat the oven to 425°.

8 Brush the edge of each crust with olive oil. Divide the pasta sauce evenly between the crusts, spreading it nearly to the edge. Sprinkle half of the Cheddar cheese onto the pizzas. Add your toppings, then top with the rest of the Cheddar and all of the mozzarella.

9 Put the baking sheet on the center oven rack. If you're using 2 sheets, stagger them on separate shelves and switch their positions halfway through baking. Bake until the cheese bubbles and the edges are golden brown, about 15 minutes.

10 Slide the pizzas onto wire racks and let them cool before slicing. Makes 12 medium slices, or 4 to 6 servings.

KIDS' STEPS Kids can proof the yeast, knead the dough, and top the pizza.

Cheesy Mexican Fondue

Surprisingly quick to prepare and good to the very last dip, fondues also have plenty of kid appeal. It's hard to beat a dinner that has the family gathered around the table dipping forkfuls of food into a simmering sauce.

INGREDIENTS

- 3 tablespoons butter
- 3 tablespoons flour
- 1/8 teaspoon garlic powder
- 2/3 cup half-and-half
- 1/2 cup chicken broth, plus more if needed
- 1 1/4 cups shredded Monterey Jack cheese (5 ounces)
- 3 tablespoons mild salsa

1 In a small saucepan, melt the butter over medium heat. Whisk in the flour and garlic powder until blended, then whisk in the half-and-half and broth. Cook and whisk until the sauce has thickened and is bubbly, about 2 minutes. Reduce heat to low.

2 Gradually add the cheese, stirring until it is melted. Stir in the salsa, if using. Transfer to a fondue pot and set the flame to keep warm.

3 Add additional chicken broth, as necessary, for desired consistency. Serve with assorted dippers (below). Makes 6 servings.

DIPPING OPTIONS

Cubes of French bread, corn bread cubes, celery and carrot sticks, jicama slices, mushrooms, red and yellow bell pepper strips, blanched broccoli and cauliflower, and/or cooked chicken cubes.

KIDS' STEPS Kids can measure the ingredients, help stir the sauce (with supervision), and prepare the dippers.

PREP TIME: **15 minutes**   COOKING TIME: **10 minutes**

Tofu Fried Rice

Not only is this dish delicious, but your child will think it's cool to cook scrambled eggs right in the middle of the other ingredients. For the best results, refrigerate the rice for several hours beforehand to keep it from turning mushy when you make the finished dish.

INGREDIENTS

2 ½   tablespoons vegetable oil

8   ounces tofu (extra firm), cut into ½-inch cubes and patted very dry

½   teaspoon sesame oil

1   teaspoon peeled, fresh grated ginger

1   garlic clove, minced

4   scallions, sliced

1   cup frozen baby peas, thawed

1   medium carrot, peeled and grated

3   cups cooked and chilled long-grain white rice

3   large eggs

2   to 4 tablespoons soy sauce

1 Heat 1 tablespoon of the vegetable oil in a large skillet, sauté pan, or wok over medium-high heat. When the oil is very hot, add the tofu, tossing it frequently, until it turns deep golden brown all over. Slide the tofu onto a large plate and set aside.

2 Heat the remaining vegetable oil and the sesame oil over medium heat. Add the ginger, garlic, scallions, peas, and grated carrot all at once. Sauté the vegetables for 1 minute, stirring them constantly. Add the cooked tofu and rice and stir the mixture occasionally as it heats for 2 to 3 minutes.

3 Beat the eggs in a small bowl. Move the rice mixture to the perimeter of the pan and pour the remaining ½ tablespoon of vegetable oil into the center. Add the eggs and stir them continuously with a wooden spoon until they are cooked, but still soft.

4 When the eggs are almost fully cooked, stir in the rice until everything is well mixed. Add the soy sauce and heat for another minute or two, stirring often. Makes 4 servings.

KIDS' STEPS Kids can cut the tofu into cubes and (with supervision) sauté the vegetables and eggs, then mix in the rice.

CHAPTER SEVEN

SIDES

Try out new tastes with an array of easy recipes

AS COMPLEMENTS TO THE MAIN ATTRACTION, side dishes are the perfect testing grounds for new flavors. Whether you're introducing your kids to an unfamiliar vegetable or a fresh herb, you have lots of freedom to mix and match ingredients. The recipes here offer new twists on old favorites, such as Grilled Mexican Corn and Armadillo Potatoes, along with more daring combinations, such as Minted Fruit Salad. Even kids who don't like veggies may be won over by sweet surprises, including Spinach Berry Salad and Candy Carrot Coins. Children can help make most of our recipes. These tips will help bring them into the kitchen.

LET KIDS PICK THE PRODUCE.
When *FamilyFun* reader Amy Nappa of Loveland, Colorado, grocery shops, she gives her son free rein in the produce aisle. The result? He's brought home — and enthusiastically eaten — brussels sprouts, eggplant, asparagus, and even carambola. He's also gained a sense of culinary adventure, which has since spread to meats, fish, and other foods.

MAKE A MEAL OF IT. There's no law that says dinner has to have a main dish. For a simple supper that's high on taste and nutrition, pair up several side dishes — such as our Cheese-Stuffed Baked Potatoes with At-Home Salad Bar, or Tortellini Salad with Easy Egg Rolls.

GO STRAIGHT TO THE SOURCE.
Take your kids to farmers markets, produce stands, and pick-your-own farms so they can see where their food comes from and meet the people who grow it. Then let them plant a garden of their own. Even if you don't have space outdoors, they can tend tomatoes or beans in a pot.

SNACK FROM THE SIDES. When your kids are ready for supper before supper's ready for them, let them dip into your dinner fixings for finger foods like cut vegetables. Turning part of the meal into an appetizer means your kids can snack away — without spoiling their appetites.

Funny-Face Salad

· ·

With a few garden vegetables, your junior chef can put a friendly smile on his salad. Hand him a plate of fresh greens. Then let him add tomato and cucumber eyes, grated carrot hair, hard-boiled egg ears, and rosy red pepper cheeks (cut with a tiny cookie cutter). Serve dressing on the side for dipping.

PREP TIME: 15 to 30 minutes

At-Home Salad Bar

For a quick and healthy appetizer or complete dinner, invite your kids to help set up a restaurant-style salad bar. The best part about a salad bar is that anything goes: fresh greens, raw veggies and toppings, leftovers, and sliced bread. For variety (and to make sure your kids eat a well-balanced meal), arrange the food in the following groups and encourage everyone to choose at least a couple of ingredients from each. Put out store-bought or homemade salad dressings (we've included a few below).

GREENS
> Romaine or iceberg lettuce, mesclun, spinach, or Swiss chard

VEGETABLE TOPPINGS
> Bell peppers, mushrooms, celery, cherry tomatoes, or carrot circles

PROTEIN ADD-INS
> Grated cheese, smoked turkey or ham cubes, salami strips, chickpeas, peanuts, pine nuts, or hard-boiled eggs

SPOON-ONS
> Croutons, pitted olives, raisins, or sunflower, pumpkin, or sesame seeds

GARDEN GREEN SALAD DRESSING

The secret to this dressing is a good, fruity extra-virgin olive oil. Measure 2 ounces balsamic vinegar and 4 ounces extra-virgin olive oil into a small sealable jar. Add ½ teaspoon salt and l minced garlic clove. Close and shake. Makes ¾ cup.

BLUE CHEESE DRESSING

This creamy, fresh-tasting blue cheese dressing is well worth the effort of making from scratch. Mix ½ cup sour cream, ¼ cup mayonnaise, 2 tablespoons milk, and 1 tablespoon lemon juice until smooth. Add ¼ cup crumbled blue cheese and salt and pepper to taste. Refrigerate overnight. Makes about 1 cup.

RANCH DRESSING

For this creamy dressing, whisk 6 tablespoons milk, ½ cup sour cream, and 1 teaspoon white vinegar in a small mixing bowl. Add ½ teaspoon garlic powder, 1 tablespoon fresh parsley flakes, ½ teaspoon fresh dill, ¼ teaspoon salt, and a touch of pepper. Chill for 30 minutes. Makes ¾ cup.

SOY-HONEY DRESSING

This light mixture can be used as a dressing or marinade. Mix 4 tablespoons soy sauce, 3 tablespoons of both water and honey, 2 tablespoons rice wine vinegar, 1 tablespoon each of sesame oil, dry or cooking sherry, and minced garlic, 1 teaspoon minced fresh ginger, and 2 scallions (white part only), chopped. Makes 1 cup.

KIDS' STEPS Kids can wash and tear the fresh greens, chop softer vegetables with a plastic knife, and place the salad bar items in bowls on the table.

Crunchy Carrot Salad

INGREDIENTS

- 1 pound carrots, peeled
- 3 tablespoons minced fresh parsley
- 2 tablespoons finely chopped fresh mint
- ¼ cup olive oil
- 2 tablespoons fresh lemon juice
- 1½ teaspoons sugar
- ¼ teaspoon salt
- ¾ cup dry-roasted unsalted peanuts

For a colorful side dish that will enliven any plate, you can't beat this light and tasty salad, which is easily multiplied for a large gathering. It will retain its delightful crunch for a day or two, so you can make it in advance — just sprinkle on a few drops of lemon juice and olive oil before serving to enhance the flavors. For best results, use California carrots, which tend to be sweeter than Canadian carrots.

1 Grate the carrots on the coarse side of a box grater (a food processor extracts a lot of liquid and will make the carrots too soft for this salad).

2 In a large bowl, gently toss together the carrots, parsley, and mint. In a small bowl, thoroughly stir together the olive oil, lemon juice, sugar, and salt, then pour the dressing onto the salad and toss again until the carrots are evenly coated. Toss in the peanuts if you are serving right away, otherwise add them right before serving so they don't soften too much.

3 Let the salad stand for 20 minutes before serving, or refrigerate it and serve within 2 days. Serves 6.

KIDS' STEPS Older kids can grate the carrots. Younger kids can mix the ingredients together.

Spinach Salad with Pine Nuts

INGREDIENTS

- ¼ cup pine nuts
- 8 slices regular or turkey bacon, cooked and crumbled
- 8 ounces baby spinach, washed and dried
- 1 can (15 ounces) mandarin oranges, drained
- Oil and vinegar-based dressing

Light, crispy, and healthful, this spinach salad is a kid and parent pleaser. "It's the only salad I can eat without a dressing," says *FamilyFun* reader Candace Pease, whose mom invented it when Candace was growing up in Santa Ana, California. The roasted pine nuts complement the bacon flavor, and the mandarin oranges add a little extra zing.

1 Heat the oven to 350°. Roast the pine nuts on a baking sheet for 5 to 8 minutes, until they turn golden brown, then allow them to cool.

2 Toss together all of the ingredients in a large salad bowl just before serving — do it any sooner and the bacon and pine nuts will lose their crispness. Serves 8.

KIDS' STEPS Kids can wash and tear the spinach, add the mandarin oranges, and toss the salad.

Spinach Berry Salad

Colorful and tasty, this salad is a snap for kids to make and delightfully refreshing with warm summer meals.

INGREDIENTS

- ½ cup vegetable oil
- ¼ cup white wine vinegar
- ¼ cup sugar
- 1 tablespoon poppy seeds
- ¼ teaspoon paprika
- ¼ teaspoon salt
- 6 ounces fresh baby spinach leaves
- 4 cups sliced strawberries

1 In a medium bowl, whisk together the vegetable oil, white vinegar, sugar, poppy seeds, paprika, and salt.

2 Combine the spinach and strawberries in a large bowl and toss well with the dressing. Serves 6.

KIDS' STEPS Kids can measure and mix the dressing, wash the spinach leaves, and slice the strawberries.

Caesar Coleslaw

INGREDIENTS

 1   cup mayonnaise

 3   tablespoons fresh lemon
     juice

 ½   teaspoon minced garlic

 1   teaspoon anchovy paste

 1   teaspoon Dijon mustard

 ½   teaspoon freshly ground
     pepper

 8   cups shredded savoy or
     green cabbage (about 1
     small head)

 2   cups shredded carrots

 4   scallions, thinly sliced

 2   cups croutons

This new take on coleslaw gets its unique flavor from anchovy paste. Make it a day before serving and leave it in the fridge to allow the dressing to soak into the salad.

1 In a large serving bowl, whisk together the mayonnaise, lemon juice, garlic, anchovy paste, mustard, and pepper to make the dressing.

2 Add the cabbage, carrots, and scallions to the bowl and toss to coat. Cover and refrigerate the salad until ready to serve. Top with croutons. Makes 6 to 8 servings.

KIDS' STEPS Kids can whisk the dressing together and toss the salad.

New Potato Salad

This old favorite gets its creamy texture not from mayonnaise, but from its mustard vinaigrette dressing combined with bits of hard-boiled egg.

INGREDIENTS

- 4   pounds new potatoes, unpeeled
- 6   tablespoons cider vinegar
- 4   tablespoons chicken broth
- 1/2   cup vegetable oil
- 3   tablespoons Dijon mustard
- 1/4   cup minced onion
- 4   hard-boiled eggs, finely chopped
- 4   stalks celery, finely chopped
- 2   teaspoons salt
-     Black pepper, to taste

1 Place the potatoes in a pot of boiling water and cook for about 30 minutes, or until tender. Do not overcook. Drain and set aside for about 20 minutes.

2 In a large bowl, combine the cider vinegar, broth, vegetable oil, mustard, onion, eggs, celery, salt, and pepper.

3 Slice the warm potatoes and toss with the dressing until well coated. Cover and let marinate for 1 hour. Refrigerate for up to 2 days. Makes 8 servings.

KIDS' STEPS Kids can wash the potatoes, mix and measure the dressing, and slice the cooked potatoes.

· ·

Minted Fruit Salad

Fresh mint gives this salad a distinctive taste that's not too overwhelming for young palates.

INGREDIENTS

- 1   cantaloupe, rind and seeds removed, cut into small pieces with a knife or melon baller
- 1   apple, cored and thinly sliced
- 1/2   pound grapes, halved
- 2   kiwis, peeled, quartered, and sliced
- 1/3   cup fresh mint, chopped, plus additional for garnish

DIRECTIONS

Combine all the fruit and toss. Just before serving, add the mint and toss again. Garnish with mint sprigs. Makes 4 servings.

KIDS' STEPS Kids can cut the fruit with plastic knives, use the melon baller, chop the mint, and toss the salad.

Pasta Salad with Fresh Herbs

This sunny pasta salad is a hit with kids and parents alike. Other fresh herbs, such as chopped dill or oregano, may be substituted for the tarragon.

INGREDIENTS

- 12 ounces rotini (corkscrew pasta)
- ¼ cup white wine vinegar
- 1 tablespoon water
- 1 ½ teaspoons salt
- ½ teaspoon sugar
- 2 teaspoons minced fresh herb leaves or ½ teaspoon dried (we used tarragon)
- ⅛ teaspoon ground black pepper
- ⅓ cup olive oil
- 2 pints red or yellow pear tomatoes or cherry tomatoes, or a combination, halved
- ¾ cup shredded carrots
- ¾ cup diced Fontina, Edam, or Swiss cheese
- ½ cup chopped fresh basil leaves

1 In a large pot of salted boiling water, cook the pasta until it's tender, about 8 minutes. Drain, rinse well, and drain again.

2 In a large bowl, whisk together the vinegar, water, salt, sugar, tarragon (or substitute herb of your choice), and pepper. Add the oil in a stream, whisking until well blended.

3 Add the pasta and the remaining ingredients to the bowl and toss well. Serve the salad at room temperature. Makes 8 to 10 servings.

KIDS' STEPS Older kids can dice the cheese and shred the carrots. Younger kids can measure and mix the dressing and toss it in with the pasta.

Tomato and Mozzarella Salad

• • • • • • • • • • • • • •

Ripe cherry tomatoes, fresh mozzarella cheese, and garden-picked basil leaves are the stars of this colorful and delicious salad. You can find fresh mozzarella, a moist, mild-flavored cheese packaged with water or whey, at the deli counter of most grocery stores.

2   to 3 tablespoons torn or chopped fresh basil leaves

½   pound fresh mozzarella (cherry size or regular, cut into bite-size pieces)

Pinch of dried oregano

Salt to taste

½   teaspoon freshly ground pepper

Pinch of hot pepper flakes (optional)

¼   cup extra-virgin olive oil

½   pound cherry tomatoes, cut in half if large

Combine the basil, mozzarella, oregano, salt, pepper, and hot pepper flakes, if desired, in the olive oil and marinate for 1 hour at room temperature. Just before serving, toss in the tomatoes. Makes 4 to 6 servings.

PREP TIME: 30 minutes   COOKING TIME: 10 minutes

Tortellini Salad

With three little boys to feed, *FamilyFun* food writer Mary King is always challenged to find a recipe that pleases everyone. One food they all love is tortellini, and this highly adaptable dinner salad lets Mary keep everyone happy. She sets aside a portion just tossed with butter, and the rest gets dressed up into a salad that can be adjusted to suit individual tastes.

INGREDIENTS

1   pound cheese tortellini

18   cherry tomatoes, cut in half

1   cucumber, thinly sliced

½   pound fresh mozzarella, cubed

2   tablespoons chopped fresh basil

1   avocado, sliced

¼   cup olive oil

Juice of 1 lime

3   tablespoons balsamic vinegar

Salt and pepper to taste

1 In a large pot, bring 3 quarts of water to a boil. Add the tortellini and gently boil for 7 to 9 minutes or until tender, then drain and rinse under cold water.

2 Transfer the cooked tortellini to a serving bowl and add the tomatoes, cucumber, cheese, basil, and avocado.

3 Mix the olive oil, lime juice, balsamic vinegar, and salt and pepper together. Drizzle it over the salad and toss to combine. Makes 6 servings.

KIDS' STEPS Older kids can peel and slice the cucumber. Younger kids can mix the dressing into the tortellini.

Easy Egg Rolls

Almost everyone likes egg rolls, and thanks to this foolproof recipe, everyone can make them. For kids, there's the fun of filling and wrapping. For parents, there's the satisfaction of watching young chefs eat the vegetables tucked inside those golden-brown shells. In addition, this recipe offers three fillings — veggie, pork, and shrimp — so you can suit the tastes of everyone in your household.

INGREDIENTS

- 1 tablespoon plus 1½ teaspoons soy sauce
- 1 tablespoon oyster-flavored sauce
- 2 teaspoons cornstarch
- 1½ tablespoons vegetable oil
- 2 teaspoons toasted sesame oil
- 2 garlic cloves, minced
- 1 cup chopped shiitake mushroom caps (about 7)
- 5 to 6 scallions, chopped
- 4 cups thinly sliced green cabbage
- 2 cups coarsely grated carrots
- ¼ teaspoon pepper
- 3 cups (or more) oil for frying
- 10 egg roll wrappers, more for variations

1 Combine the soy sauce, oyster sauce, and cornstarch in a small bowl. Whisk until the cornstarch is dissolved and the mixture is smooth. Set the bowl aside.

2 Heat the vegetable oil and sesame oil in a large skillet set over high heat. Cook the vegetables in order, stirring often: First add the garlic and cook for 2 minutes. Add the mushrooms and scallions and cook for 1 minute. Then add the cabbage and carrots and cook for another minute. Finally, add the cornstarch mixture and cook for 1 minute. Stir in the pepper.

3 Transfer the vegetables to a plate. Cool thoroughly, about 30 minutes.

4 Pour about 1 inch of oil into a deep skillet or pan set over medium heat (the oil will need to come about halfway up the sides of the egg rolls when frying). While the oil heats (about 10 minutes), assemble the egg rolls as shown at right: set a wrapper diagonally on your work surface. Spread ¼ cup of filling onto the center of it, leaving a 1½-inch border on each side. Fold the corner nearest you over the filling, then the 2 sides over the center. Moisten the edge of the remaining corner with a wet fingertip. Tightly roll the egg roll toward the moistened edge and press to seal. Repeat the process with the remaining wrappers.

5 When the oil is hot enough, around 350°, reduce the heat to medium-low. Using long-handled tongs, carefully lower 4 or 5 egg rolls at a time (or as many as your skillet will hold) into the hot oil. Fry until golden brown, about 5 minutes, then turn them over and fry for about 5 minutes more. If they are browning too quickly, reduce the heat and allow the oil to cool for a couple of minutes before frying the next batch.

6 Transfer the fried egg rolls to a paper towel-lined plate and let them cool slightly. Serve them with your favorite duck or plum sauce. Makes 10 egg rolls.

PORK AND VEGGIE EGG ROLLS

Brown ⅓ pound of lean ground pork in a medium skillet set over high heat until it's no longer pink, about 3 minutes, breaking up the pork with a wooden spoon. Push the meat to the sides of the pan, then follow the directions for the Easy Egg Rolls. Adjust the flavor by adding ½ teaspoon or more of soy sauce according to taste.

SHRIMP AND VEGGIE EGG ROLLS

Follow the recipe for the Easy Egg Rolls, then add 1 cup of chopped cooked shrimp at the end. Adjust the flavor by adding ½ teaspoon or more of soy sauce.

KIDS' STEPS Kids can measure and mix the sauce and fill and roll the egg rolls.

Grilled Mexican Corn

INGREDIENTS

6   medium ears of corn

4   tablespoons butter (or 2 tablespoons each of butter and olive oil)

SPICE MIX

½   teaspoon ground cumin

½   teaspoon ground coriander

½   teaspoon ground oregano or basil

½   teaspoon chili powder

Dash each of cayenne and paprika

½   teaspoon salt

Seasoned with spiced butter, this grilled corn makes plain boiled corn pale in comparison. Plus, your kids will think it's really cool to cook the ears right in their husks. Soaking the ears beforehand is key, as it provides the moisture needed to steam the corn while it grills.

1 Pull back the husks on the corn as far as you can without removing them altogether. Remove the silk, then push the husks back into place. Soak the ears in a sink full of water for an hour. If you're at a campsite, you can place them in a plastic bag along with enough water to cover them and turn the bag occasionally.

2 When the fire is hot and you're ready to start grilling, melt the butter (or butter and oil) in a small pan. Stir in all of the spice mix ingredients.

3 Remove the corn from the water and pull back the husks again. Brush each ear with the seasoned butter (or plain melted butter for kids or adults who may not like the spice), then put the husks back in place.

4 Using long-handled tongs, set the corn on a grate over your fire where the heat is intense. Grill the corn for about 15 minutes, turning it every 3 to 4 minutes. Don't worry if the husks scorch. Remove the corn from the grill and let it cool for a few minutes before eating. Makes 6 servings.

KIDS' STEPS Kids can remove the silk from the ears of corn and brush the kernels with the spiced butter.

....

Smoky Rice and Beans

INGREDIENTS

1   tablespoon olive oil

½   cup diced onion

½   teaspoon ground cumin

1   teaspoon minced chipotle (sold in the international food aisle of the grocery store)

1   cup uncooked white rice

1   cup cooked black beans, drained and rinsed

½   cup diced tomatoes

½   cup corn (optional)

2   cups chicken broth

2   tablespoons chopped scallion greens (optional)

The secret ingredient in this rice dish is chipotle (smoked jalapeño peppers). Just a touch of these peppers gives this dish a slight smoky flavor.

1 Heat the oil in a medium saucepan over medium heat. Add the onion, cumin, and chipotle. Cook for 5 minutes, stirring occasionally, or until the onion starts to soften.

2 Add the rice and stir to coat with the oil. Add the black beans, tomatoes, and corn, if desired. Season with salt and pepper. Add the chicken broth and bring to a boil. Reduce the heat to low, cover, and simmer for about 25 minutes or until all the liquid is absorbed.

3 Remove from the heat and let stand for 10 minutes. Transfer to a serving bowl, then sprinkle with scallions, if desired. Makes 4 to 6 servings.

KIDS' STEPS Kids can rinse and drain the beans and measure the rice and corn.

Food for Thought

PREP TIME: 35 minutes   **COOKING TIME:** about 25 minutes

Zucchini Canoes

The zucchini in this recipe resemble mini dugout canoes. The zesty bread crumb cargo is flavored with chopped veggies and bits of pepperoni or crisp bacon.

INGREDIENTS

- 4   zucchini
- 2   tablespoons olive or vegetable oil
- 1   medium onion, chopped
- ¾   cup chopped mushrooms
- 1   clove garlic, minced
- 2   cups diced fresh tomatoes
- 2   tablespoons chopped fresh parsley
- ¼   teaspoon salt, plus more to taste
- ⅓   cup dry bread crumbs
- ¼   cup grated Parmesan cheese
- 2   to 3 tablespoons finely chopped pepperoni (pork or turkey) or crisp-cooked bacon (optional)

1 Fill a large soup pot halfway with water and add 2 teaspoons of salt. Bring the water to a boil and cook the zucchini whole for 1½ minutes, just enough to tenderize the shells. Use metal tongs to transfer them to a colander until they are cool enough to handle.

2 Halve the zucchini lengthwise. Scoop out the flesh with a spoon, being sure to leave an outer wall about ⅓ inch thick. Finely chop the flesh and set it aside.

3 Measure the oil into a large sauté pan. Add the onion and zucchini flesh and sauté over moderate heat, stirring often, for 5 minutes. Add the mushrooms and garlic. Sauté for 2 more minutes.

4 Add the tomatoes and turn up the heat slightly. When the mixture reaches a low boil, cook for 2 to 3 minutes, until the tomatoes are soft. Remove the pan from the heat, then stir in the parsley, salt (at least ¼ teaspoon), and a little pepper. Let the vegetables cool for several minutes, then add the bread crumbs, cheese, and, if desired, pepperoni or bacon.

5 Heat the oven to 400° and grease a shallow, medium baking dish with 1 tablespoon of vegetable oil. Spoon the filling into the zucchini halves and arrange them in the baking dish.

6 Bake the Zucchini Canoes on the center oven rack until heated through, about 20 to 25 minutes. Serve right away. Makes 4 to 6 servings.

KIDS' STEPS Kids can scoop out the zucchini flesh, chop it up, and fill the boats with the bread crumb mixture.

TIP: When scooping out the flesh, be sure to leave at least a ⅓-inch wall so the zucchini boat is sturdy enough to hold the bread crumb mixture.

Asparagus Salad with Sweet Pepper Confetti

Fresh asparagus gets gobbled up — warm or cold — with this sweet pepper dressing. The dressing tastes great on salads too, so feel free to make extra to keep on hand.

INGREDIENTS

- ⅓ cup olive oil
- 2 tablespoons red wine vinegar
- 1 teaspoon Dijon or grainy mustard
- 2 cloves garlic, minced
- ½ teaspoon salt
- ¼ teaspoon pepper
- 2 pounds asparagus
- ¼ red bell pepper, diced
- ¼ yellow bell pepper, diced

KIDS' STEPS Kids can measure and mix the dressing, pour it on the asparagus, and sprinkle on the pepper pieces.

1 Combine the oil, vinegar, mustard, garlic, salt, and pepper in a small screw-top jar or cruet. Shake it and set it aside.

2 To serve the asparagus cold, have a large bowl of ice water by the side of the stove. Bring a medium pot of lightly salted water to a rapid boil over high heat. Plunge the asparagus into the boiling water. Cook until it is tender but still firm, about 2 to 4 minutes after the water returns to a simmer, depending on the thickness of the asparagus. Drain and plunge the asparagus into the ice water. After about 5 minutes, drain and pat dry.

3 Place the asparagus with the tips pointing in the same direction, then drizzle with the dressing and sprinkle with the pepper pieces. If serving warm, drain the asparagus thoroughly after boiling and lay it out directly on the platter. Makes 4 to 6 servings.

Candy Carrot Coins

Tossed with a brown sugar and butter glaze, these carrots taste slightly sweet and look perfectly shiny.

INGREDIENTS

- 1 pound carrots
- 1 tablespoon butter
- 2 tablespoons brown sugar
- 1 teaspoon water

1 Peel the carrots, then slice each one into rounds. Steam or boil the carrots until tender but not mushy, about 10 minutes. Drain the carrots from any water they are in and set them aside.

2 In a small frying pan, melt the butter, stir in the brown sugar and water, and cook for 1 minute. Add the carrots and toss to coat. Cook on low for 3 to 4 minutes or until the carrots are thoroughly glazed. Makes 4 servings.

KIDS' STEPS Use this recipe as an opportunity to teach your child how to peel and slice carrots, use a microwave, and make a glaze.

PREP TIME: **about 10 minutes**   BAKING TIME: **about 1 hour 10 minutes**

Cheese-Stuffed Baked Potatoes

INGREDIENTS

- 4   medium potatoes
- 1   cup grated extra-sharp Cheddar cheese
- 1/4   cup grated Parmesan cheese
- 1/2   cup sour cream
- 2   to 4 tablespoons butter
- 1/2   cup minced onion
- 2   garlic cloves, minced
  Salt to taste

These mashed potatoes, packed inside a crunchy skin, can be baked along with a roasted chicken or oven roast. Four potatoes should be enough for six to eight people, since you're cutting the potatoes in half and the filling is rich.

1 Heat the oven to 400°. Wash the potatoes and pierce each one a few times with a fork. Bake until done, about 1 hour. Leave the oven on.

2 Split the freshly baked potatoes in half while they're still hot. Carefully scrape the insides into a large bowl, saving the skins.

3 Add the cheeses, sour cream, butter, onion, and garlic. Mash well and add salt to taste.

4 Stuff the mixture back into the potato skins. Return the potatoes to the oven and bake until the tops are golden brown. Makes 6 to 8 servings.

KIDS' STEPS   Kids can scrub the potatoes and pierce them with a fork, then help mash and stuff them after they are cooked.

PREP TIME: **10 minutes**   COOKING TIME: **20 minutes**

Mashed Potatoes

According to our kid testers, mashing the cooked potatoes with an old-fashioned potato masher is the best part of making this classic side dish. For a garnish, top each cloud of mashed potatoes with a homemade herbed butter pat (at right).

INGREDIENTS

- 4   large russet or Idaho potatoes (about 2 ½ pounds)
- ½   cup milk
- 3   tablespoons butter

1 Using a vegetable peeler, remove the skin from the potatoes and use the tip of the peeler to scoop out any brown spots. Cut each potato in half lengthwise and then slice into ½- to 1-inch pieces. Place the potatoes in a saucepan and cover with cold water.

2 Bring the potatoes to a boil, watching carefully to make sure they do not boil over. Once they have come to a boil, cook for an additional 10 minutes or until tender, about 20 minutes in all. (While the potatoes are boiling, make the butter pats at right, if you like.) Take the pan of potatoes off the stove and drain the water.

3 Pour the milk over the potatoes and add the butter. Using a potato masher, press down on the potatoes until they are smooth. (If you are working with younger kids, transfer the potatoes from the hot saucepan to a large bowl before mashing.)

4 Spoon the mashed potatoes onto the dinner plates and serve with a pat or two of regular or herbed butter. Serves 4.

KIDS' STEPS   Kids can wash and peel the potatoes, then mash them after they are cooked.

FUN FOOD
Herbed Butter Pats
. . . .

Decorate your mashed potatoes with pats of butter flecked with herbs and cut into fun shapes.

To make them, mix together 4 tablespoons of softened butter and 1 teaspoon of dill or chives. Press the mixture into a 2- by 3-inch rectangle on a piece of waxed paper. Place in the freezer for about 10 minutes, then use miniature cookie cutters to cut out butter pats. Keep the cutouts on a chilled plate (so they won't melt) until just before serving.

Armadillo Potatoes

Bring a little western flavor to your table with these taters. The bread crumb stripes are what help these spuds pose as the hard-backed critters.

INGREDIENTS

- ¼ cup bread crumbs
- ¼ cup grated Parmesan cheese
- 1 tablespoon paprika
   Olive oil
- 1 teaspoon salt
- ½ teaspoon pepper
- 6 Idaho potatoes, peeled and cut in half lengthwise

1 Heat the oven to 450°. In a bowl, mix together the bread crumbs, cheese, paprika, 1 tablespoon of olive oil, salt, and pepper. Set the mixture aside.

2 Transform each potato half into an armadillo by cutting 9 or so notches ½ to ¾ inch deep in the rounded top. For each armadillo, cut a square of aluminum foil big enough to loosely wrap around it, brush the center with olive oil, then place the potato on it, flat side down. Sprinkle the top with some of the crumb mixture, pressing it into the grooves, then seal the potato in the aluminum foil.

3 Arrange all of the foil-covered potatoes on a baking sheet and bake them for about 40 minutes. Open the pouches carefully — they will be hot and full of steam. Makes 10 to 12 servings.

KIDS' STEPS Kids can fill the slits in the potatoes with the crumb mixture and wrap the potatoes in the foil.

Oven-Baked Steak Fries

These fries are a snap to make, and much more nutritious than the fast-food version. Kids can jazz them up with melted cheese or spicy seasonings.

INGREDIENTS

- 4 medium Idaho potatoes
- ¼ cup oil
   Salt to taste

1 Heat the oven to 425°. Peel the potatoes and slice them into about 10 wedges. Dry off any excess starch with paper towels.

2 In a baking dish, toss the potatoes with the oil to coat. Bake for 25 minutes, turning at least once. Add salt to taste. Makes 4 servings.

CHEESE FRIES Melt grated cheese over fries.

SPICY FRIES Sprinkle your favorite spices (cayenne, seasoning salt) over fries before baking.

ITALIAN FRIES Melt mozzarella over baked wedges and dip in tomato sauce.

THANKSGIVING FRIES Serve your fries with gravy.

KIDS' STEPS Older kids can peel and cut the potatoes. Younger kids can toss them in oil and season.

CHAPTER EIGHT

DESSERT

Hook your kids on cooking with a fun finale

SWEETS ARE A MAIN THEME in many of our favorite childhood memories — a birthday cake with fanciful icing, an ice-cream cone on a summer night, or a blueberry pie at a family celebration. The recipe is simple: Want to hook a child on cooking? Start with dessert. They'll enjoy every step — from the first lick of batter to the last dinner-table compliment. The recipes in this chapter are perfect for parties, potlucks, or family suppers. For an extra serving of kid appeal, try these tips.

INSPIRE A KITCHEN ARTIST. Let your kids' imaginations run wild by cooking up one of our playful desserts in this chapter. They can bake and decorate the funny-face Cookie Puppets. Or help them to create the cow (or pig or sheep) cake using our simple design. The possibilities are endless. And best of all, every masterpiece is edible.

OFFER A SWEET INCENTIVE. *FamilyFun* reader Ruth Gill of Cheney, Washington, motivates her children to do their chores by putting one dry ingredient of a cookie recipe in a large covered bowl for each day they complete their work. When all the fixings are there, the kids add the liquid ingredients and bake up a batch as a reward.

THINK BIG. Is it your turn to bring snacks to the scout meeting, sports event, or school party? This chapter is brimming with surefire hits that are easy to bake in bulk. For a satisfying blend of substance and style, check out our Peanut Butter Balls. Keep the crew busy by letting them decorate their own To-Dye-For Cupcakes, or score a touchdown with our Sporty Cookies.

START A NEW TRADITION. The Duggar children of Tallahassee, Florida, celebrate each birthday with a giant, number-shaped cookie honoring their age. Before eating it, they pose for a keepsake photo with the timely treat.

Simple Sugar Cookies

We've tried a lot of sugar cookie recipes over the years and found this one to be the best. It holds its shape when baked so kids can have fun making different cutouts, like the trains shown above.

MY GREAT IDEA
On a Roll

• • • • • • • • • • • • • • • • • • • •

"My kids love to bake cookies but there isn't always time to make the dough from scratch. When time allows, I make a triple batch of cookie dough. I keep out enough for one batch, then roll the other two into 'cookie logs,' wrap them in plastic wrap, and freeze them.

"When we want to make cookies, I just pull out a log from the freezer and the kids get to roll their own dough balls and place them on the sheet.

"For my 4-year-old daughter, Aubrey, I put a little extra flour in the dough and she can make cookie sculptures or cut out shapes with cookie cutters. My younger son Spencer, age 2, just likes to pat the dough onto the sheet.

"By making the dough myself (versus purchasing the store-bought cookie dough) I can monitor the ingredients and make healthier versions."

— *Brook Hampton*
Plainville, Connecticut

INGREDIENTS

1	cup unsalted butter, softened
¾	cup sugar
1	large egg
1	teaspoon vanilla extract
¼	teaspoon salt
2½	cups flour

1 Heat the oven to 375°. Using an electric mixer at medium-high, cream the butter, gradually adding the sugar. Beat in the egg until evenly mixed, then blend in the vanilla extract and salt.

2 With a wooden spoon, stir the flour into the creamed ingredients, about one third at a time, until evenly blended. The dough may seem soft, but it will firm up when refrigerated.

3 Divide the dough in half. Flatten each portion into a disk and seal in plastic wrap. Refrigerate until firm.

4 Cover a sturdy baking sheet with aluminum foil and lightly coat the foil with cooking spray. Between 2 sheets of waxed paper lightly dusted with flour, roll the dough to a ¼-inch thickness. Remove the top sheet.

5 Cut out the cookies with a cookie cutter. Use a spatula to transfer the shapes to the baking sheet, leaving about an inch between cookies.

6 Bake until the cookies start to brown lightly around the edges, about 10 minutes. Let the cookies cool on the baking sheet for 5 minutes, then transfer them to wire racks to cool completely.

7 To prevent sticking, line your serving plate or tin with waxed paper and place additional waxed paper between layers. Makes about 3 dozen cookies.

COLORFUL COOKIES To color the dough, separate it into as many pieces as the colors you want to make. To each piece, add food coloring, drop by drop, until you reach the desired hue. Knead the dough to distribute the color evenly.
TRAIN VARIATION From lightweight cardboard, cut train templates about 2- by 3½-inches to look like the cars above. Set the templates on rolled-out cookie dough. With the point of a sharp knife (adults only), cut out the cars. Bake the dough as directed above. Using frosting, attach LifeSavers candies for wheels, licorice strings to connect the train cars, and edible pretzel cargo.

KIDS' STEPS Kids can mix and measure the cookie dough, roll it out, and cut it into fun shapes.

Sporty Cookies

Your child is sure to get a kick out of decorating these sugar cookies. An empty can serves as the perfect cookie cutter for both the soccer and football shapes.

INGREDIENTS

- Simple Sugar Cookies dough (recipe at left)
- Butterscotch chips
- White sprinkles
- White frosting
- Black decorators' gel

1 Heat the oven to 375°. For the soccer cookies, use an empty can to cut out round shapes from the rolled-out dough. For the football cookie shapes, cut the bottom off the can as well, and squash it a bit to make it an oval-shaped cookie cutter. Bake all the cookies on a cookie sheet until the edges start to brown, about 10 minutes.

2 Leave the soccer cookies on the sheet for 2 to 3 minutes, then transfer to a wire rack to cool completely.

3 While the football cookies are still warm, sprinkle 10 to 15 butterscotch chips on each one. Once the chips soften, spread them like icing over the cookie surface, then add a row of sprinkles to the center to resemble football lacing.

4 For the soccer balls, spread the frosting on each cooled cookie, then use a toothpick to etch five-sided panels in it. With the gel, trace over the lines and fill in a few of the shapes, as shown. Makes about 2 dozen cookies.

KIDS' STEPS Kids can roll out the dough, cut out the cookies, and decorate with the frosting.

··

Cookie Puppets

Kids will have a blast turning their sugar cookies into puppets on a stick.

INGREDIENTS

- Simple Sugar Cookies dough (recipe at left)
- 15 to 18 lollipop sticks
- Assorted candies
- Frosting

1 Heat the oven to 375°. Roll the dough to ¼ inch thick, then use a cookie cutter or a widemouthed glass to cut out round shapes.

2 Place each cookie on an ungreased baking sheet, insert a lollipop stick in the center of each, and bake until they are golden brown around the edges, about 8 to 10 minutes.

3 Once the cookies have cooled, let the kids add facial features using assorted candies. Then, fill a pastry bag with frosting and use a writing tip to add eyes, a mouth, or a mop of hair.

KIDS' STEPS Kids can press the sticks into the cookies and decorate the faces.

Peanut Butter Balls

Stick-to-your-ribs Peanut Butter Balls keep well for up to a week, so make them with the kids over the weekend and let them munch on them all week. Serve them plain or dipped in a number of tasty toppings.

INGREDIENTS

1   cup smooth peanut butter

½   cup honey

¼   cup toasted wheat germ

1   cup crisped rice cereal

   Toppings, such as shredded coconut, finely chopped nuts, toasted wheat germ, melted chocolate, or crushed graham crackers

1 Cover a baking sheet with waxed paper. In a medium bowl, stir together the peanut butter, honey, wheat germ, and rice cereal until well blended.

2 Roll the mixture into balls. (Ours are about 1 inch in diameter.) If your dough is too sticky to work with easily, add a little more cereal or place it in the refrigerator until it stiffens up.

3 If you like, put one (or more) of the toppings listed in a small bowl and roll or dip the balls into it (to dip them in melted chocolate, first spear each one on a fork).

4 Place the balls on the waxed paper and chill them for about 2 hours. Store those coated in wheat germ in the refrigerator; store all others in the refrigerator or at room temperature. Makes about 2 dozen balls.

KIDS' STEPS   Older kids can help stir the mixture and dip the balls into the chocolate. Younger ones can roll the balls in the different toppings.

Old-Fashioned Peanut Butter Cookies

Our kid testers loved rolling this dough into balls and using the tines of a fork to press the distinctive crosshatch pattern into the cookies. Once baked, these classic treats are moist and loaded with rich, peanutty flavor, making a welcome lunch box dessert or after-school snack.

INGREDIENTS

- ¾ cup butter, at room temperature
- ¾ cup brown sugar, packed
- ½ cup sugar
- 1 cup peanut butter (creamy or crunchy)
- 2 eggs
- 1½ teaspoons vanilla extract
- 2 cups flour
- ½ teaspoon baking soda
- ½ teaspoon baking powder
- ¼ teaspoon salt

1 Heat the oven to 350°. In a large mixing bowl, use an electric mixer to cream the butter. Add the sugars to the butter and cream them together. Beat in the peanut butter. Then add the eggs one at a time, mixing until combined. Mix in the vanilla extract.

2 In a medium mixing bowl, stir together the flour, baking soda, baking powder, and salt. Gradually add the flour mixture to the peanut butter mixture and stir until thoroughly combined.

3 Lightly flour your hands, then roll a heaping tablespoon of cookie dough into a 1½-inch ball. Place the ball on an ungreased cookie sheet. Continue until you have placed about 9 balls on the cookie sheet, about 1½ to 2 inches apart.

4 Press the tines of a fork into the balls, both to flatten the dough and to create decorative patterns on the cookie.

5 Bake until the cookies are lightly brown around the edges, about 10 to 12 minutes. Repeat in batches until you have used all the cookie dough. Makes about 3 dozen cookies.

KIDS' STEPS Kids can roll cookie dough into balls and press the fork patterns into them.

TIP: To create the classic peanut butter cookie stamp, lightly press the tines of a fork into the ball, then turn the fork 90° and press down again.

Giant Cowboy Cookies

These oversize cookies combine favorite trail mix ingredients with a classic oatmeal cookie. The precise flavor — from M&M's to dried fruit — is the chef's choice.

INGREDIENTS

1½   cups flour

1   teaspoon baking powder

½   teaspoon baking soda

¼   teaspoon salt

1   cup butter, at room temperature

¾   cup brown sugar

½   cup granulated sugar

2   eggs

1   teaspoon vanilla extract

2   cups rolled oats

2½   cups mix-ins: semisweet chocolate chips, M&M's, chopped walnuts or other nuts, and/or raisins or other dried fruit

1 Heat the oven to 350°. In a large bowl, mix together the flour, baking powder, baking soda, and salt. In a separate bowl, cream together the butter and sugars, then beat in the eggs. Stir in the vanilla extract, then stir in the flour mixture.

2 Fold in the rolled oats until thoroughly combined. Select and measure 2½ cups (total) of your favorite mix-ins, then fold the choices into the dough.

KIDS' STEPS   Older kids can crack the eggs and help mix the batter. Younger kids can choose the mix-ins and fold them into the dough.

3 Use a ¼-cup measuring cup to transfer the cookie dough onto an ungreased baking sheet (you'll be able to fit about 6 on a sheet). Wet the bottom of a wide glass and press it onto each cookie to flatten it (alternatively, you can flour the bottom of the glass). Bake until lightly browned, about 15 minutes. Transfer the cookies to a cooling rack and let cool. Makes about 2 dozen cookies.

Molasses Cookies

FamilyFun reader Julie Jones used to make these cookies with her Aunt Erma when she was a child. Today, she enjoys telling stories about her beloved aunt while passing the recipe on to her children, who love to roll the cookies in sugar before baking them.

INGREDIENTS

- ³/₄ cup vegetable shortening
- 1 cup packed light brown sugar
- ¹/₄ cup molasses
- 1 egg
- 2 cups flour
- 2 teaspoons baking soda
- ¹/₄ teaspoon salt
- 1 teaspoon ground cinnamon
- 1 teaspoon ground cloves
- 1 teaspoon ground ginger
- ¹/₂ cup sugar

1 In a large mixing bowl, cream together the shortening, brown sugar, molasses, and egg. In a separate medium bowl, sift together the flour, baking soda, salt, and spices. Gradually add the dry ingredients to the creamed mixture, blending after each addition, until the dough is evenly mixed.

2 Heat the oven to 375°. Put the ½ cup of sugar in a medium bowl. Using floured hands, shape the dough into balls the size of whole walnuts. Roll the balls in the sugar, then place them on a large, lightly greased baking sheet, leaving a couple of inches between them.

3 Bake for 8 to 9 minutes. Cool the cookies on the baking sheet for 1 minute before transferring them to a cooling rack. Makes about 2 dozen cookies.

KIDS' STEPS   Older kids can mix and add the dry ingredients. Younger ones can help form the dough into balls, roll them in the sugar, and place them on the cookie sheet.

Shamburgers

INGREDIENTS

- 2   sticks butter, softened
- 1   cup sugar
- 2   eggs, plus 1 for the cookie glaze
- 1   teaspoon vanilla extract
- 2 1/2   cups flour
- 1 1/2   teaspoons baking powder
- 1/2   teaspoon salt
- 2   tablespoons sesame seeds
- 1   cup shredded coconut
-      Green food coloring
-      Red and yellow icing (in a tube)
- 12   large or 36 medium peppermint patties

On April Fools' Day, serve up dinner — or is it dessert? — with this unexpected treat. When your kids take a bite, their taste buds will be pleasantly deceived by the no-beef peppermint patties, special sauce, and sesame cookie buns.

1 Heat the oven to 375°. Use an electric mixer to cream the butter and the sugar until fluffy. Add 2 eggs and beat well. Stir in the vanilla extract. Sift the flour, baking powder, and salt into a separate bowl. Then, add the dry ingredients to the creamed mixture and blend well.

2 For large "buns," drop the dough by rounded tablespoons onto a lightly greased baking sheet at least 1 inch apart (for medium buns, drop the dough by rounded teaspoons), then use the bottom of a floured glass to lightly press the dough into a circle. Beat the remaining egg and use a pastry brush to spread it on top of each cookie. Sprinkle sesame seeds on the tops. Bake the large cookies for 10 minutes and the medium ones for 8 minutes, or until they are golden brown.

3 To make the "lettuce," place the shredded coconut into a plastic bag and add a few drops of green food coloring to it. Close the bag and shake it until the coconut has turned a light green.

4 To assemble the "burgers," choose two cookies that are about the same size and shape. Spread icing "ketchup" or "mustard" on the bottom bun, add an appropriately sized peppermint patty, and sprinkle on coconut lettuce. Add a squirt of icing ketchup or mustard to hold the top bun in place.

5 Arrange the Shamburgers on a platter or wrap in foil like the fast food restaurants do. Makes approximately 12 large or 36 medium burgers.

KIDS' STEPS Kids can mix the cookie dough, make the coconut "lettuce," and add the frosting "ketchup" and "mustard."

Edible Eagles

INGREDIENTS

- 6   large marshmallows
- 1/4   cup white chocolate chips
- 1   package finely shredded coconut
- 6   chocolate-covered Oreo cookies
- 6   whole cashews
-      Black decorators' gel

Send your family's taste buds soaring with a nest of these bald eagle treats.

1 Use a toothpick to make a hole in the side of the marshmallow (you'll fit the cashew nose in here later). Melt the chips on the stovetop or in the microwave.

2 For each bird, drop a marshmallow into the melted chocolate and coat it well, then roll it in the coconut, leaving one end uncovered.

3 Immediately set the marshmallow, coconut-free end down, atop a cookie and let the chocolate set. Insert the cashew beak and add black decorators' gel eyes. Makes 6 eagle treats.

KIDS' STEPS Kids can roll the chocolate-coated marshmallows in the coconut and set them on the cookies.

Best Fudge Brownies

Few kids can pass up the chance to bake a batch of brownies, and this recipe is especially irresistible. Made with generous measures of chocolate, butter, and sugar, it yields the fudgiest bars ever tasted.

INGREDIENTS

- ¾ cup unsalted butter
- 8 ounces semisweet or bittersweet chocolate, coarsely chopped
- 1 cup sugar
- 1 cup firmly packed light brown sugar
- 4 large eggs, at room temperature
- 2 teaspoons vanilla extract
- 1½ cups flour
- ½ teaspoon salt
- 1 cup chopped walnuts or pecans (optional)

1 Heat the oven to 350°. Cut the butter into ½-inch pieces and place them in the top of a double boiler over barely simmering water. As the butter melts, sprinkle the chocolate evenly into it. Leave the mixture over the heat for 5 minutes, then stir or whisk it until smooth. Transfer the top of the double boiler to a cooling rack and let the chocolate cool to room temperature.

2 Lightly butter a 9- by 9-inch square cake pan (do not use a smaller pan) and dust it with flour, knocking out the excess.

3 Combine the sugars in a large mixing bowl, using your fingers to break up any lumps. Add the eggs. Beat the eggs and sugar until well blended — about 30 seconds — with an electric mixer set on medium-high. Blend in the vanilla extract. Add the cooled chocolate (which should still be liquid) and mix on medium speed just until evenly blended.

4 Sift the flour and salt into a medium bowl, then stir them into the chocolate mixture, about half at a time, until no streaks of flour remain. Stir in the nuts, if desired. Then scrape the batter into the prepared pan and smooth it with a spoon.

5 Bake the brownies on the center oven rack for 30 to 35 minutes. When done, the brownies will have risen slightly and the top will have a thin, brittle crust. Do not overbake. For the best results, use 3 toothpicks to test for doneness. Insert one into the brownies about 1 inch from the side; it should come out clean. A second toothpick inserted 2 inches from the side should have a little batter stuck to it, and a third, inserted in the center, should be coated with a bit more batter than that.

6 Transfer the pan to a wire rack and cool the brownies thoroughly. To get the cleanest cuts, cover and refrigerate the brownies for several hours before slicing (provided you can resist that long). Serve slightly cool or at room temperature. Makes 12 to 16 brownies.

KIDS' STEPS **Kids can butter the pan, sift the flour, crack the eggs, and stir the batter.**

PREP TIME: 25 minutes   **BAKING TIME:** about 20 minutes

Brownie Cupcakes

Portable and peanut-buttery delicious, this muffin-cup brownie is perfect for lunches, bake sales, or parties. These bake even faster than the pan brownies, so you'll want to be careful not to overbake them.

INGREDIENTS

1	batch Best Fudge Brownies batter (at left), made without nuts
⅓	cup smooth peanut butter
1½	ounces cream cheese, softened
1	egg
¼	cup sugar

1 Line 18 to 20 cups of a muffin pan with bake cups. Combine the peanut butter, cream cheese, egg, and sugar in a medium bowl and beat them with an electric mixer until evenly blended. The texture should be like whipped peanut butter. If it's not stiff enough, add a little extra peanut butter.

2 Fill each muffin cup about halfway with brownie batter. Spoon about 2 teaspoons of peanut butter filling into the center, pushing it down slightly into the batter. Cover the filling with another spoonful of batter, making sure that the cups are no more than about two thirds to three quarters full.

3 Bake just until well risen and cracked on top, about 20 minutes. Then transfer the pans to a wire rack and cool for 30 minutes. Remove the brownies from the pan and place them directly on the wire rack to finish cooling (they'll sink as they do) before serving. Makes 18 to 20 brownies.

KIDS' STEPS Kids can line the muffin tins with bake cups and fill with brownie batter, then add the peanut butter mix.

TIP: Push the peanut butter mix into the first layer of brownie batter, then top with a second layer of brownie batter.

FUN FOOD
Brownie Pizza

Topped with red frosting "sauce" and grated white chocolate "cheese," this looks like a real pizza but tastes like a decadent dessert.

1	box brownie mix
	White frosting
	Red food coloring paste
	White chocolate
	Assorted toppings, such as white chocolate, shredded coconut, chocolate cookie pieces, and M&M's

Prepare the brownie recipe according to the box directions, with one exception: instead of pouring the mixture into a baking pan, pour it into a lightly greased 12-inch pizza pan. Bake at 350° for 20 to 30 minutes or until a knife inserted in the middle comes out clean. Let the brownie cool completely.

While the brownie cools, mix up some red frosting "sauce" by adding red food coloring paste, ½ teaspoon at a time, to the vanilla frosting until you reach the desired shade (think tomato sauce). Spread the sauce over the cooled brownie pie, then add your toppings.

For "cheese," roughly chop or grate (adults only) white chocolate or sprinkle on shredded coconut. Then let the kids add their favorite candy toppings.

Little Helpers

PREP TIME: 10 minutes   BAKING TIME: about 45 minutes

Lemon Squares

With lemon filling and a buttery shortbread crust, these classic bars offer the perfect combination of sweet and tart.

SHORTBREAD

³⁄₄	cup butter, at room temperature
1 ¹⁄₂	cups flour
¹⁄₂	cup confectioners' sugar

FILLING

2	to 3 lemons
4	eggs
1 ¹⁄₂	cups sugar
¹⁄₄	cup flour

1 Heat the oven to 350°. For the shortbread crust, use a wooden spoon to work the butter, flour, and confectioners' sugar in a large bowl until the mixture holds together. Transfer the dough to an ungreased 9- by 13-inch pan and press the mixture into the pan. Bake until the edges begin to brown, about 20 minutes.

2 While the shortbread is baking, make the lemon filling. Wash and dry the lemons, then grate 2 tablespoons of the rinds using the small holes on your grater (see tip below). Slice each lemon in half and squeeze out ¹⁄₃ cup of juice. Remove any seeds.

3 In a large mixing bowl, whisk the eggs and the sugar together. Whisk in the flour. Stir in the lemon zest and juice. Pour the filling over the baked shortbread and return the pan to the oven until the filling no longer jiggles and the edges are lightly brown, about 25 minutes. Cool, then dust with confectioners' sugar. Makes 24 two-inch lemon squares. Refrigerate any leftovers.

KIDS' STEPS   Younger kids can pat the shortbread crust into the pan. Older kids can grate the lemon to get the zest.

TIP: To grate a lemon, hold the grater firmly with one hand and grip the lemon with the other, keeping fingers as far away from the grater as possible.

Yellow Cake

Cakes made from scratch take just a few extra steps from the boxed variety, and the rich, fresh flavor is well worth the effort. Use this recipe to make a sheet cake, 2 round cakes, or 24 cupcakes.

INGREDIENTS

- ¾ cup butter, at room temperature
- 1½ cups granulated sugar
- 3 eggs
- 3 cups flour
- 2 teaspoons baking powder
- ¼ teaspoon salt
- 1⅓ cups buttermilk
- 2½ teaspoons vanilla extract

1 Heat the oven to 350°. Prepare a 9- by 13- by 2-inch pan, two 9-inch round pans, or two 12-cup cupcake pans by greasing them and dusting them with flour.

2 Cream the butter and sugar until light and fluffy. Add the eggs one at a time, beating well after each addition.

3 In a large bowl, sift together the flour, baking powder, and salt. In a separate bowl, mix together the buttermilk and vanilla extract.

4 Mix (but don't overmix) a third of the flour mixture into the butter mixture. Then mix in half the buttermilk mixture followed by another third of the flour mixture, the rest of the buttermilk, then the last of the flour mixture.

5 Pour the mix into the prepared pans and bake until a toothpick inserted into the center comes out clean (for the 9- by 13- by 2-inch pan, about 45 minutes; the 9-inch round pans, about 30 minutes; and the cupcake pans about 15 minutes). Serves 10 to 12.

KIDS' STEPS Older kids can measure and mix the batter. Younger kids can spread on the frosting.

PREP TIME: 20 minutes   BAKING TIME: 20 to 45 minutes

Chocolate Cake

For the chocolate lover in your family, this recipe takes the cake. Top your sheet cake, round cakes, or cupcakes with one of the flavored frostings listed at right.

INGREDIENTS

1½	cups water
4	ounces unsweetened chocolate
⅓	cup cocoa powder
1	cup canola oil
3	eggs
1	teaspoon vanilla extract
1	cup granulated sugar
¾	cup packed brown sugar
2½	cups flour
1½	teaspoons baking soda
1	teaspoon baking powder
¼	teaspoon salt

1 Heat the oven to 350°. Prepare a 9- by 13-inch pan, two 9-inch round pans, or two 12-cup cupcake pans by greasing them and dusting them with flour.

2 In a microwave-safe liquid measuring cup, measure 1½ cups water. Add the unsweetened chocolate to the water. Microwave for 2 to 3 minutes or until the chocolate has melted, stirring after

1½ minutes. Transfer to a medium bowl and whisk until smooth. Whisk in the cocoa and set the mixture aside.

3 Using an electric mixer on high speed, beat the oil, eggs, vanilla extract, and granulated and brown sugars for 2 to 3 minutes, or until light and fluffy.

4 In a separate bowl, stir together the flour, baking soda, baking powder, and salt. Add the flour mixture and chocolate mixture alternately to the oil mixture, stirring well after each addition. When all the ingredients are added, beat on medium for 1 minute.

5 Pour the mix into the prepared pans and bake until a toothpick inserted into the center comes out clean (for the 9- by 13- by 2-inch pan, about 45 minutes; the 9-inch round pans, about 30 minutes; and the cupcake pans about 15 minutes). Serves 10 to 12.

KIDS' STEPS Older kids can measure and mix the batter. Younger kids can grease the pans and spread frosting on the cake.

TIP: To prepare the pans, butter them well, then add a tablespoon of flour to one. Rotate and tap the pan to distribute the flour evenly. Repeat the process with the other pan.

This homemade frosting is quick and easy to prepare. Plus, it can be flavored in any way you (or the birthday child) fancy.

1	cup unsalted butter, at room temperature
3½	cups sifted confectioners' sugar
1	teaspoon vanilla extract
2	to 4 tablespoons milk

With an electric mixer, beat the butter, sugar, and vanilla extract at low speed. Add in the milk bit by bit until the mixture has reached a spreadable consistency. Makes about 3 cups.

CHOCOLATE FROSTING
Substitute 1 cup of cocoa powder for 1 cup of the confectioners' sugar.

LEMON FROSTING
Substitute lemon extract for the vanilla extract and add the finely grated zest of 1 lemon. Substitute ½ to 1 tablespoon of lemon juice for the milk.

CREAM CHEESE FROSTING
Substitute 4 to 6 ounces of cream cheese for ½ cup of the butter. Beat in an additional ½ to 1 cup of confectioners' sugar.

STRAWBERRY OR RASPBERRY FROSTING
Add ¼ cup of seedless strawberry or raspberry jam to the basic frosting recipe.

Birthday Tradition

• • • • • • • • • • • • • • • •

"For each of our three children — Tom, 11, Ruth, 9, and Sam, 5 — we have a photo album of their birthday cakes. We all enjoy looking at the pictures (remember the year Sam wanted a dog and got a dog cake?). The albums have turned into a record not just of the cakes, but of our children's changing interests as they grow."

— *Meg Ryan*
Florence, Massachusetts

DECORATING TIME: **20 minutes**

Sleepover Cake

One of our favorite things to do at *FamilyFun* is construct fun and original cake creations. The Sleepover Cake is one of our (and our readers') favorites.

INGREDIENTS

- 1 baked 13- by 9- by 2-inch cake
- 4 cups pale pink frosting
- 2 cups pink frosting
- 5 Twinkies
- 5 marshmallows
- 5 vanilla or chocolate wafer cookies
-    Gel icing (pink and green)
-    Mini jawbreakers
-    Pink and green Fruit by the Foot

1 Turn the cooled cake upside down and spread a thin layer of pale pink frosting on it. Then frost a pink sheet on the top third of the cake.

2 To make the bodies, slice the Twinkies in half lengthwise and place the tops cut-side down on the cake bed as shown. Flatten the marshmallows for pillows, and position the wafer faces on them (curly hair and big smiles can be made with gel icing; mini jawbreakers are perfect for eyes).

3 Frost a pale pink blanket over the Twinkies. To make flowers, use pink and green gel icing. Cut Fruit by the Foot and ruffle it to make a snappy bed skirt.

KIDS' STEPS **Kids can frost and decorate** the Sleepover Cake in the likeness of their friends.

Animal Cakes

The idea for this menagerie of cakes came from *FamilyFun* reader Michelle Fehlman. She needed a cake for her son Andrew's first birthday party that was both easy to make and big enough to feed her Phelan, California, family of ten.

BASIC CAKE

- 1   baked dome cake
- 1   baked round cake
- 3   cupcakes (4 for the pig)

PIG DECORATIONS

- 2   to 3 cups pink icing
- 2   green Hi-C Fruit Slices (hooves)
- 1   pink Hi-C Fruit Slice (mouth)
- 2   Jujubes (nose)
- 2   Jujyfruits (eyes)
     Red shoestring licorice (ears and eyelashes)
- 1   red Sour Belt (tail)

SHEEP DECORATIONS

- 2   to 3 cups white icing
- 1   cup chocolate icing
- 3 1/2   cups mini marshmallows
- 2   Jujyfruits (eyes)
- 1   nonpareil (nose)
     Red shoestring licorice (mouth)

COW DECORATIONS

- 2   to 3 cups white icing
- 1   cup chocolate icing
- 2   malted milk balls (eyes)
- 2   black gumdrops (nose)
- 1/2   red Hi-C Fruit Slice (mouth)
- 1   pink Hi-C Fruit Slice, cut into 4 pieces (ears)
     Black shoestring licorice (hooves and eyelashes)

DIRECTIONS: Set the dome cake upside down in the center of the round cake and secure with icing, as shown. Cut 1 cupcake in half and place it as shown for the ears, then arrange 2 more cupcakes as legs.

PIG: Frost the cakes and cupcakes pink and decorate as shown, then add a cupcake snout.

SHEEP: Frost the cakes (except for a triangular face area), the outsides of the ears, and the top halves of the hooves with the white icing, then cover with mini marshmallows. Use a pastry bag (or a plastic bag with one corner cut off) to pipe small dollops of chocolate icing onto the face, bottom halves of the hooves, and centers of the ears. Decorate as shown.

COW: Frost the cakes and cupcakes with white icing, adding random chocolate icing "spots." Decorate as shown.

KIDS' STEPS Kids can frost the cakes and make the animal designs with the assorted candies.

DECORATING TIME: 10 minutes

Flutter Delight

When Robert Davis of Stoughton, Massachusetts, studied butterflies in second grade, his mom, *FamilyFun* reader Lonnie, dreamed up this class treat to tie in with the theme.

INGREDIENTS

- Baked cupcakes
- White icing
- Sour gummy worms
- Candy fruit slices, sliced in half
- Gumdrop slices (optional)
- Shoestring licorice

DIRECTIONS: Frost each cupcake. Arrange ½ gummy worm for the body, the fruit slices for wings (attach a gumdrop detail with icing, if you like), and small pieces of shoestring licorice for the antennae.

KIDS' STEPS Kids can frost the cupcakes and create the butterflies with the pieces of candy.

··

DECORATING TIME: 10 minutes

Tic-Tac-Yum

Kim Arant from Lawrenceville, Georgia, sent us this idea for a quick game of cupcakes. It's the perfect decorating project for a younger child and an excellent centerpiece for a game-themed party.

INGREDIENTS

- 10 baked cupcakes
- Frosting
- 5 sour rings (or LifeSavers)
- 10 1½-inch pieces of Twizzlers Pull-n-Peel candy
- 4 orange Starburst Fruit Twists
- 4 yellow Starburst Fruit Twists

DIRECTIONS: Frost the cupcakes. Place a sour ring O on five of the cupcakes. Make an X with the Twizzlers Pull-n-Peel candy on the remaining five. Place the yellow and orange Starburst Fruit Twists in a tic-tac-toe grid and arrange the cupcakes.

KIDS' STEPS Kids can frost the cupcakes, make the tic-tac-toe board out of the strip candy, and decorate the cupcakes.

DECORATING TIME: **10 minutes**

To-Dye-For Cupcakes

Deanne Nutaitis of Wilkes-Barre, Pennsylvania, was so inspired by the tie-dye theme for her daughter's birthday that she dyed the tops and the insides of these cupcakes. Simply fold colored nonpareils into cupcake batter and bake as directed.

INGREDIENTS

28 baked cupcakes (to make the peace sign)

White icing

Gel icing in a tube (4 or 5 colors)

Toothpick

DIRECTIONS: Frost the cupcakes, then squirt a series of concentric circles of different-colored gel icings on each one. To create the tie-dye effect, draw a toothpick through the gel, moving from the center outward like a spiderweb. Arrange the cupcakes into a peace sign, as shown.

KIDS' STEPS Kids can frost the cupcakes and draw the toothpick through the colors to create the tie-dye effect.

DECORATING TIME: **10 minutes**

Froggy Fun

Kids will be leaping over each other to make this simple bullfrog cupcake that shows the amphibian peeking out of its watery hideaway.

INGREDIENTS

Baked cupcakes

Light blue frosting

Large green gumdrops

White chocolate chips

Black decorators' gel

DIRECTIONS: For each frog, frost a cupcake a watery blue. Then, slice a large green gumdrop in half. Press the tip of a white chocolate chip into the cut surface of each half, centering it near the bottom edge. Squirt a dab of black decorators' gel onto each chip. Then press the frog eyes into the frosting.

KIDS' STEPS Kids can frost the cupcakes, push the chips into the split gumdrops, and dab on the decorators' gel.

Carrot Cake

Filled with finely grated carrots and crushed pineapple, then spread with a smooth coating of cream cheese icing, this classic dessert will be a fun treat for your aspiring baker to make.

CAKE

- 1 ¼ cups flour
- 1 cup sugar
- 1 teaspoon baking soda
- ½ teaspoon baking powder
- ½ teaspoon salt
- ½ teaspoon each of cinnamon, nutmeg, and ground ginger
- ¼ teaspoon ground cloves
- 3 large eggs
- ¾ cup vegetable oil
- 1 teaspoon vanilla extract
- 1 ¼ cups finely grated carrots
- ½ cup finely chopped walnuts
- ½ cup chopped raisins

ICING

- 12 ounces regular cream cheese, at room temperature
- 4 tablespoons butter, softened
- 1 ½ teaspoons vanilla extract
- 3 to 3 ½ cups sifted confectioners' sugar
  Food coloring

FILLING AND GARNISH

- ¾ cup crushed pineapple, well drained
- 1 ½ cups sweetened flaked coconut (optional)

1 To prepare two 8- by 2-inch round cake pans, first trace around one of the pans to create 2 waxed paper circles. Lightly grease the pans and line them with the cutout circles. Grease the papers and dust the pans with flour, knocking out the excess. Heat the oven to 350°.

2 Sift together the flour, sugar, baking soda, baking powder, salt, and spices into a large bowl. Make a well in the center and add the eggs, oil, and vanilla extract.

3 Using an electric mixer on low speed, beat the liquids briefly in the well, then blend the entire batter on low just until evenly mixed.

4 Using a rubber spatula, fold the carrots, walnuts, and raisins into the batter until evenly mixed. Divide the batter between the cake pans.

5 Bake the cakes on the center oven rack for about 25 minutes, until a toothpick inserted into the center of the cakes comes out clean. Transfer the pans to a large cooling rack and cool the cakes (in the pans) for 10 minutes.

6 Run a butter knife around the edges of the cakes to loosen them, then remove each cake from its pan by inverting it onto a wire rack. Peel away the waxed paper and let the cakes cool completely (at least 1 hour) before icing them.

7 While the cakes are cooling, make the icing. Using an electric mixer, beat the cream cheese and butter in a bowl until smooth. Blend in the vanilla extract. Add the confectioners' sugar, about 1 cup at a time, beating until smooth and fluffy after each addition. Reserve about ⅔ cup of the icing, dividing it between 2 small bowls. Cover and chill the bowls.

8 Place the first cake layer on a serving plate. Smooth a generous layer of the icing over the top (if the icing is too soft, chill it for about 30 minutes before continuing). Then spread the crushed pineapple over the icing.

9 Place the second layer on top of the first, then ice the top and sides of the cake. Cupping some of the coconut in one hand, gently pat it onto the side of the cake, working your way all around the perimeter.

10 Dye one of the reserved batches of frosting orange and the other green. Use a pastry bag to pipe carrots on top of the cake. Store the finished cake in the refrigerator until you plan to serve it, then let it sit at room temperature for 20 to 30 minutes before slicing. Makes 8 to 10 servings.

KIDS' STEPS Kids can sift the dry ingredients, dye the frosting, and pat on the coconut.

Watermelon Parfaits

Served in **parfait glasses** to show off each luscious layer, these colorful ice cream-and-sherbet creations are a treat for both your eyes and taste buds.

INGREDIENTS

- 1   pint lime sherbet
- 1   pint vanilla ice cream
- 1   pint raspberry sherbet or sorbet
-     Chocolate chip morsels

1 For each parfait, pack lime sherbet into the bottom of a parfait glass, at an angle as shown, if you like. Chill the glass in the freezer for 5 to 10 minutes so the sherbet will harden.

2 Add a thin layer of vanilla ice cream (to complete the rind) and chill for another 5 to 10 minutes.

3 Complete the parfait with a generous layer of raspberry sherbet or sorbet. For a festive effect, press a row of chocolate chips against the glass midway through the layer, as shown. Top the parfait with a few more chocolate chips. Makes 4 parfaits.

KIDS' STEPS Kids can scoop the sherbet and cover the parfaits with the chocolate chips.

....

Colossal Ice Cream Sandwich

INGREDIENTS

- 1   roll (18 ounces) refrigerated cookie dough
- 4   cups ice cream (any flavor)
-     Plastic wrap
-     Aluminum foil

In this irresistible two-in-one dessert, cookies and ice cream come together for a treat that's big enough to satisfy a crowd.

1 Heat the oven to 350°. Generously spray two 9-inch round cake pans with cooking spray (to insure that the cookies don't stick to the pan after cooking).

2 Cut the dough into twenty ½-inch slices and lay 10 pieces in each pan. Press the dough slices together, leaving a ¾-inch gap around the edge of the pan. Bake for 14 minutes or until golden, then let them cool in the pans for 2 minutes.

3 Remove the cookies (without breaking them, if possible) and place them on wire racks to cool completely.

4 Place 2 pieces of plastic wrap at right angles to each other in one of the cooled pans, leaving enough overhang to cover the sandwich. Set one of the cookies upside down in the pan and spread 4 cups of slightly thawed ice cream over it. Add the second cookie (right side up), then wrap the sandwich with the plastic.

5 Cover the pan with aluminum foil and place it in the freezer until the ice cream is firm (about 5 hours). To serve, use a serrated knife (parents only) to slice the sandwich into 8 wedges.

KIDS' STEPS Older kids can help cut the cookie dough. Younger kids can press the slices into the pans.

Apple Crumble

Easier to make than pie but every bit as delicious, apple crumble has a cinnamony oatmeal topping that perfectly complements autumn's sweet-tart fruit. Tried and true, this recipe guarantees young chefs great results and makes plenty.

APPLE FILLING

- 8 to 9 cups peeled, cored, and sliced apples (about 7 to 8 large apples), preferably Granny Smiths or Fujis
- 3 tablespoons sugar
- 1 tablespoon lemon juice

OATMEAL TOPPING

- 1 cup flour
- ½ cup old-fashioned rolled oats
- ⅓ cup sugar
- ⅓ cup packed light brown sugar
- ½ teaspoon cinnamon
- ¼ teaspoon salt
- ½ cup cold unsalted butter, cut into ¼-inch pieces
- ½ cup chopped pecans or walnuts (optional)

1 Heat the oven to 375°. Generously grease a shallow, 13- by 9-inch casserole with soft butter.

2 Pile the sliced apples in the casserole. Sprinkle the sugar and lemon juice over them and stir the fruit gently, right in the pan. Once the slices are evenly coated, spread them uniformly.

KIDS' STEPS   Kids can stir together the apples, sugar, and lemon juice in the baking pan and press the crumb topping onto the apples.

3 Combine the flour, oats, sugar, brown sugar, cinnamon, and salt in a large mixing bowl. Toss the ingredients with your hands to mix.

4 Add the butter pieces to the dry ingredients and use your fingers to rub in the butter until you have pea-size crumbs. At this point, none of the flour should be noticeable. Mix in the pecans or walnuts, if desired.

5 Spread the topping evenly over the apples and press it down gently with your palm. Bake the crumble on the center oven rack for 45 to 50 minutes, until juice bubbles around the edges and the topping is golden brown. If the top starts to get too brown, move the crumble down one shelf.

6 Transfer the crumble to a wire rack and cool for at least 15 minutes before serving. Makes 9 to 12 servings.

Blueberry Pie

This is a great starter pie for teaching kids to bake. The lemon-tinged blueberry filling is a snap to toss together, and the flaky piecrust is a classic that you can use for any flavor pie. Of course, kids will think the cookie-cutter stars are the tops to make.

PIECRUST

- 3 cups flour
- 2 tablespoons sugar
- 1 teaspoon salt
- ½ cup cold unsalted butter
- ½ cup cold vegetable shortening
- 8 tablespoons ice-cold water

FILLING

- 6 cups blueberries, washed and stemmed
- 2 teaspoons grated lemon zest
- 2 tablespoons fresh lemon juice
- 6 tablespoons flour
- ¾ cup sugar

1 To make the crust, whisk together the flour, sugar, and salt in a large mixing bowl. Cut the butter and shortening into ¼-inch pieces and toss them into the dry ingredients by hand to evenly distribute them. Now use a pastry cutter to cut them into the flour until they are the size of small peas.

2 Sprinkle in half of the water and toss well with a fork. Add the remaining water a teaspoon at a time until the pastry will pack into a ball.

3 Knead the dough once or twice, then divide in half. Place each half on a large sheet of plastic wrap and flatten them into ¾-inch-thick disks. Wrap the disks in the plastic and chill them for about 1 hour. You can chill them longer, but they may get too firm; just let them sit at room temperature for 5 to 10 minutes before rolling.

4 Working atop a sheet of lightly floured waxed paper, roll each disk into a 12-inch circle with a flour-dusted rolling pin. Put one back in the refrigerator, and invert the other one over a 9-inch pie pan and peel off the paper. Gently fit the pastry into the pan without stretching it and pinch the edge

into a fluted rim. Chill in the freezer for 15 minutes before using.

5 Heat the oven to 375°. Place the blueberries in a large bowl and sprinkle with the lemon zest, lemon juice, flour, and sugar. Toss gently until the berries are evenly coated.

6 Pour the filling into the crust. Cut the remaining dough into shapes with cookie cutters. Lay the shapes, touching one another, on top of the filling. Press any pieces that meet the sides of the crust into the edges.

7 Place the pie pan on a foil-lined tray (to catch any spills) and bake in the lower third of the oven for 1 hour or until the filling is bubbly around the edges and the crust is lightly browned. Serve hot, warm, or at room temperature. Serves 8.

KIDS' STEPS Kids can cut and roll the dough, make the blueberry filling, and punch stars (or other shapes) out of the dough with a cookie cutter.

TEACHING KIDS TO COOK
How to Make a Piecrust

Avoid overworking the dough. A layered, flaky crust is created by flattening the butter, not breaking it up into tiny pieces.

Place the rolling pin in the center of the dough and roll out toward, but not over, the edges. Rotate the pin every few rolls.

To crimp the dough, pinch it with your forefinger and thumb and use your other forefinger to make an indentation.

Classic Apple Pie

It's never too early to teach a child to bake apple pie. The pie's flaky crust and juicy cinnamon filling will be just desserts for his baking efforts.

INGREDIENTS

- 6 to 8 apples, such as Granny Smith, Cortland, Rome, or a local variety of tart apples
- Juice of half a lemon
- ¾ cup sugar
- 1 teaspoon cinnamon
- ¼ teaspoon nutmeg
- 2 tablespoons flour
- 2 rolled-out pie dough disks (see recipe, page 213)
- 2 tablespoons butter, cut into chunks
- Milk (for glaze)

1 Heat the oven to 425°. Peel, core, and slice the apples into ¼-inch pieces. Place them (about 6 cups) in a large mixing bowl. Pour the lemon juice over the apples, then the sugar, cinnamon, nutmeg, and flour. Toss well.

2 Gently lay one of the dough disks into a pie pan and pinch the edges. Spoon the spiced apples into the pan and dot with the butter. Place the second dough disk loosely on top of the apple mixture and cut slits in it to allow the steam to escape. Brush the top with milk for a glaze.

3 Bake for 45 minutes or until the crust is golden brown and the juices are bubbling. (Put a sheet of foil on the rack under the pie to catch any spills.) If the crust begins to brown before the pie is fully baked, cover it with foil.

4 Let the pie cool, then serve with a scoop of vanilla ice cream or a slice of Cheddar cheese. Serves 8.

KIDS' STEPS Older kids can peel and slice the apples. Younger kids can crimp the piecrust and brush on the glaze.

Pumpkin Pie

Let your kids personalize this classic pumpkin pie with a handprint turkey.

INGREDIENTS

- 2 rolled-out pie dough disks (see recipe, page 213)
- 1 can (16 ounces) packed pumpkin
- 1 can (14 ounces) sweetened condensed milk
- 2 eggs
- 1 teaspoon apple pie spice
- 1 cup semisweet chocolate chips (optional)
- Sugar, for top

1 Heat the oven to 375°. Have your child trace her handprint on a piece of lightweight cardboard, then cut it out to create a stencil. Place the stencil over one of the pie dough disks and cut around it, adding turkey feet to the bottom of the hand.

2 Place the dough cutout on a nonstick baking sheet, brush with water, then sprinkle with sugar. Bake for 8 minutes or until golden brown. Let cool.

3 Place the remaining dough disk in a 9-inch pie pan. Gently press the crust against the side and bottom of the pan and crimp the edges.

4 In a large bowl, combine the pumpkin, milk, eggs, and spice and mix until smooth. Stir in the chocolate chips, if desired, then pour into the piecrust and bake until an inserted knife comes out clean (except for the chocolate), about 35 to 40 minutes. Place the baked turkey cutout in the center of the pie and allow the pie to cool before serving. Serves 8.

KIDS' STEPS Kids can add the turkey legs to the handprint, crimp the crust edge, and mix the pumpkin filling.

PREP TIME: 1 hour   BAKING TIME: about 10 minutes   CHILLING TIME: at least 6 hours

Banana Cream Pie

With its sweet graham cracker crust piled high with layers of vanilla pudding, sliced bananas, and whipped cream, this pie seems custom-made for kids.

GRAHAM CRACKER CRUST

1 3/4 cups fine graham cracker crumbs

1/2 teaspoon cinnamon

Big pinch of salt

6 tablespoons melted butter

1 teaspoon water

VANILLA PUDDING FILLING

3/4 cup plus 2 tablespoons sugar

1/4 cup plus 2 tablespoons cornstarch

1/8 teaspoon salt

3 cups milk or half-and-half

3 egg yolks

2 tablespoons butter, cut into pieces

2 teaspoons vanilla extract

WHIPPED CREAM AND GARNISH

1 1/4 cups very cold heavy cream

2 tablespoons confectioners' sugar, sifted

2 large ripe bananas (not too ripe)

Chocolate for garnish

1 Heat the oven to 325°. Lightly butter a deep 9- or 10-inch pie pan. In a large mixing bowl, combine the graham cracker crumbs, cinnamon, and salt and mix the ingredients briefly. Stir in the melted butter and water with a fork. Then use your fingers to rub together the mixture until the crumbs are uniformly moistened.

2 Empty the crumbs into the prepared pie pan. Press them evenly into the bottom and about three quarters of the way up the side. Bake the piecrust on the center oven rack for 8 minutes, then cool it in the pan on a rack while you make the filling.

3 Combine the sugar, cornstarch, and salt in a nonstick medium saucepan and whisk them until evenly blended. Then whisk in the milk and the egg yolks.

4 Heat the pudding over medium heat, stirring continuously until it thickens and bubbles, about 5 minutes. Continue cooking for 1 minute more, whisking all the while to keep it from boiling.

5 Remove the pan from the heat and whisk in the butter one piece at a time. Add the vanilla extract and whisk several more times. Immediately pour the filling into the piecrust, spreading and smoothing it with a wooden spoon.

6 Gently press a piece of plastic wrap against the filling to keep a skin from forming. Put the pie on a cooling rack and cool to room temperature, then chill it for at least 6 hours, or overnight.

7 Ten minutes before assembling the pie, chill a mixing bowl and the beaters you'll use to make the whipped cream. Beat the heavy cream in the cold bowl until soft peaks form. Add the confectioners' sugar and continue to beat with a whisk until it is stiff but still smooth.

8 Remove the plastic covering from the pie and use a rubber spatula to spread a thin layer of whipped cream over the pudding. Quarter the bananas lengthwise, then cut them crosswise into small chunks, letting them fall over the pie in a single layer.

9 Mound the remaining whipped cream on top of the sliced bananas. Then garnish with shaved chocolate, if you like, and refrigerate the pie until serving time. Makes 8 to 10 servings.

KIDS' STEPS Kids can press the crust into the pie plate, pour the pudding onto the crust, and slice the bananas on top.

Graham Cracker Chalet

As any builder will tell you, gingerbread house construction is traditionally tricky. But not so with this Alpine chalet. Made from a revolutionary new building material — graham crackers — it's a cinch for even first-time home builders.

MATERIALS

- Craft knife and scissors
- Cardboard six-pack container
- Masking tape
- Yellow cellophane
- Flashlight
- Corrugated cardboard
- Frosting
- Graham crackers
- Pretzel nibs, vanilla wafers, and assorted candies for decorating (see opposite page)
- Golden Grahams cereal

BASIC STRUCTURE: Using a craft knife (a parent's job), cut out windows on the long sides of the six-pack. Tape a square of cellophane inside each window. From one of the short sides, cut out a door to one side of the center seam. To make sure the flashlight will fit inside, try putting it through this door (cut out some of the inner structure so you can center the light).

Using the six-pack as a guide, outline and cut out of the corrugated cardboard a peaked wall for each short side (see below). From one peaked wall, cut out a hinged door in the same place as the one on the container. Tape both cardboard walls in place. Cut out a 12- by 9-inch piece of cardboard, then fold it in half for the roof. Lay it on top of the container, trimming if necessary, and tape in place.

SIDING: Starting at the front of the house and ending with the roof, apply icing to each surface using a butter knife, then press on graham crackers (see above). **TIP:** Leave a ¼-inch margin along the bottom of the house. The crackers may settle as they dry. Resize any crackers that don't fit by nibbling!

TRIM: Now you can decorate your house however you like, using icing to affix the decorations. We used rows of pretzel nibs and vanilla wafer cookies on the walls, accented with mini marshmallows and licorice-twist trim.

ROOF: Cover one side of the roof with icing. Apply the bottommost row of Golden Grahams, then overlap each successive layer, working upward. Repeat for the other side. Add a licorice ridgepole.

For the chimney base, cut 2 Starburst candies in half diagonally and attach them to the roof with icing mortar. Top with more Starburst bricks. Use scissors to cut long, thin triangles from the large marshmallows. Attach these along the eaves with icing.

FINAL TOUCHES: Add any other decorations you like, such as starlight mint ornaments, a LifeSavers wreath, or confectioners' sugar snow. Allow all frosting to dry, then turn on the flashlight and slide it inside the house.

KIDS' STEPS Kids can frost the cardboard house, tile the roof with the cereal, and decorate the house with candy.

Home Sweet Home

For more exterior decorating of your chalet, try the ideas below — or head to the candy aisle and dream up your own.

GUMDROPS Set these out as boulders and shrubs or join with pretzel sticks to make a low fence. Or, use them as the heads and bodies of penguins and skiers (for the skiers, attach licorice limbs with toothpicks).

RED HOT CANDIES Perfect for tree decorations, holly berries, and house trim.

CARAMELS Use these as stepping-stones or stack them up to make a stovepipe. You can also put two atop stacked wafer cookies for a moose's head. (Toothpicks make great spindly legs, and circus peanuts great hooves.)

FRUIT ROLL-UP Roll this out as a pathway or cut it to make flags and banners.

SWEDISH FISH Layer these as roof tiles or stand them on end as a colorful fence.

STARBURSTS Great for brick paths, fences, or wishing wells.

PRETZEL STICKS Pile up as firewood or use for fencing, roofing, or siding.

LICORICE LACE Outline doors and windows or string up as holiday lights.

MARSHMALLOWS Pile up a few as a snowbank or stack together three for a snowman.

NECCO WAFERS These colorful disks make great siding, roof tiles, flagstones, and penguin wings.

SKITTLES Use these to make house trim, holiday lights, roof tiles, or doorknobs.

GRAHAM CRACKERS Great for shutters, pathways, skis, docks, and signs.

SUGAR CONES Coat these with a thin layer of icing and roll in green sugar to make a pine tree.

JELLY BEANS Great for snowman or penguin noses and skiers' hands and feet.

Index

Index

Index

PAGE 67